BENOÎT GALLOT

Translation by
ARIELLE AARONSON

With original artwork by
DANIEL CASANAVE

THE SECRET LIFE OF A CEMETERY

THE WILD NATURE AND ENCHANTING LORE OF PÈRE-LACHAISE

GREYSTONE BOOKS
Vancouver/Berkeley/London

First paperback edition 2026
First published in English by Greystone Books in 2025
Originally published in French as *La Vie secrète d'un cimetière*, copyright © 2022 by
Les Arènes, Paris. Published by special arrangement with Les Arènes, France, in conjunction
with their duly appointed agents Books and More Agency and 2 Seas Literary Agency
English translation copyright © 2025 by Arielle Aaronson
Photographs copyright © 2022 by Benoît Gallot

26 27 28 29 30   5 4 3 2 1

The publisher expressly prohibits the use of *The Secret Life of a Cemetery* in
connection with the development of any software program, including, without
limitation, training a machine-learning or generative artificial intelligence (AI) system.

All rights reserved, including those for text and data mining, AI training, and similar
technologies. No part of this book may be reproduced, stored in a retrieval system,
or transmitted, in any form or by any means, without the prior written consent of the
publisher or a license from The Canadian Copyright Licensing Agency (Access Copyright).
For a copyright license, visit accesscopyright.ca or call toll free to 1-800-893-5777.

Greystone Books Ltd.
greystonebooks.com

Cataloguing data available from Library and Archives Canada
ISBN 978-1-77840-390-3 (pbk.)
ISBN 978-1-77840-158-9 (cloth)
ISBN 978-1-77840-159-6 (epub)

Editing for English edition by Paula Ayer
Proofreading by Crissy Boylan
Cover and text design by Fiona Siu
Cover images by Andrew_Howe (crow); Andrea_Hill (robin);
duncan1890 (scarce swallowtail); bauhaus1000 (wildflowers) / istockphoto.com;
Pierre-Yves Beaudouin (statue) / Wikimedia Commons
Illustrations by Daniel Casanave

Printed and bound in Canada on FSC® certified paper at Friesens. The FSC® label
means that materials used for the product have been responsibly sourced.

Greystone Books thanks the Canada Council for the Arts, the British Columbia Arts
Council, the Province of British Columbia through the Book Publishing Tax Credit,
and the Government of Canada for supporting our publishing activities.

The translation of this work was supported by the Centre National du Livre.

EU Safety Information: Easy Access System Europe, Mustamäe tee 50,
10621 Tallinn, Estonia, gpsr.requests@easproject.com.

Greystone Books gratefully acknowledges the xʷməθkʷəy̓əm (Musqueam),
Skwxwú7mesh (Squamish), and səlilwətaɬ (Tsleil-Waututh) peoples on
whose land our Vancouver head office is located.

*For Colombe, Zacharie,
Sacha, Rose, and Camille*

◇◇◇◇◇

WE WALKED THROUGH the cemetery, remarking on the graves. Florence began to bristle at the meticulously polished headstones, all the shiny marble surfaces she found ugly. I mean, that's not my style at all. I want to be buried in some forgotten cemetery with crumbling graves overgrown with weeds, crosses leaning every which way, and foxes and wild goats who slip in at night.

PIERRIC BAILLY, *Le Roman de Jim*

Contents

Translator's Note xi
Preface xiii

16, Rue du Repos
1

Tombstone Tourism
11

Life at the Cemetery
23

The Flagship
33

The Funeral Bug
44

Fashion Victims
53

An Unusual Job
63

A Stroll Among the Graves
71

Bubbles of Hope
83

The Tissue Box
88

You Can't Outfox a Fox
100

Time to Celebrate
108

Living Among the Dead
120

Ghost Stories
130

Under the Parisian Sky
142

The Legend of Jim
152

No Dead-End Jobs Here
157

VIP Treatment
171

The Same World
183

Dying Is Really the
Last Thing to Do
196

Glossary of Funerary Symbols 207
Acknowledgments 213
Notes 217
Bibliography 219

Translator's Note

IN 1804, NAPOLEON issued a set of reforms that revolutionized the burial system in France. Under the new laws, cemeteries became public spaces whose land was owned and managed by municipal governments. Individuals had the opportunity to lease grave space as part of an arrangement known as a "concession." Concessions can be temporary (defined as five to fifteen years), long-term (thirty or fifty years), or perpetual—i.e., forever. Once a temporary concession expires, the land is repossessed by the government, the bodies exhumed and the remains sent to an ossuary, and the grave space recycled for a new occupant.

The term "concession" refers to an agreement governing a piece of land that has been leased by the government to an individual for burial purposes. The more generic "plot" refers to any space within a cemetery where someone is buried.

Because almost all grave spaces in France are governed by concession agreements, the two terms have been used interchangeably.

Preface

WITH EACH PASSING year, there is growing speculation among scholars and industry professionals that cemeteries as we know them today will cease to exist in the not-so-distant future. Indeed, people seem disenchanted with these familiar spaces scattered throughout their cities and towns. Visits to cemeteries are decreasing. In France, reasons for this phenomenon may include inaccessibility, a decline in religion, and a rise in cremation rates—up from 1 percent in the 1980s to nearly 40 percent today. I'd like to add another reason, one that is more personal and revealing of the present moment: entering a cemetery means having to confront the reality of death.

Death remains taboo because it eludes us; it is a certainty over which we have no control. Billionaires may well strive to make humans immortal—by the end of the century, no less!—but until we triumph over death, our only alternative is to brush it aside or even excise it from our language, resorting to familiar euphemisms such as "departed," "passed on," or "lost." Only dramatic, violent, or unusual deaths are given media coverage, sometimes leading to marches or vigils. Ordinary, everyday death is kept hidden nowadays. At a time when life expectancy continues to rise and nine people out of ten die outside the home, it is possible to live into old age and never see a dead body. Gone are the days when families gathered for the wake of a loved one, when it was customary to hang black mourning drapes on buildings to announce a death, when cars pulled over to let funeral processions pass. Faced with this distance, with this gradual erasure of death, will cemeteries be the final holdouts before they, too, are wiped off the map?

I believe their loss would be an absolute tragedy—not only because I live and work in one, or even because I come from a long line of funeral industry professionals. I love cemeteries because I am convinced that, far from the sad, bleak places we imagine them to be, most are soothing spaces full of unexpected riches.

◇◇◇◇

TO BE HONEST, when I was first put in charge of managing a cemetery, I didn't see much beyond my duties. These involved overseeing burials, making sure graves received the respect they were due, and ensuring proper maintenance, which at the time meant eradicating the slightest weed. It took a 2011 decision by Paris City Council to change both my methods and my attitude. Goodbye pesticides, hello wild plants and animals! As the walkways gradually greened over and weeds started popping up between the graves, a new ecosystem began to emerge. The cemetery I managed was no longer a place of death alone. Right before my eyes, it was becoming a haven of biodiversity for local plants, insects, birds, and even mammals.

In dense urban areas where it isn't always possible to create new green spaces, an increasing number of cities have reimagined their cemeteries to include roles beyond their primary function. The land can double as parks, cultural venues, and even unofficial nature reserves. For years, we turned away from cemeteries out of a fear of death. Now, the return of life may suddenly rescue them from the brink of extinction.

◇◇◇◇

MY JOB AS curator has taken on a whole new dimension, with each day bringing new discoveries. The most incredible occurred on April 23, 2020. In a shuttered-up and locked-down Paris, as the bodies of COVID-19 victims arrived daily at the gates of Père-Lachaise, I crossed paths with a fox cub! It was a miraculous discovery. The moment I posted the photograph to social media, the press went into a frenzy. It didn't take long before the snapshot wound up on the front page of *Le Parisien*. I can't take any credit for shining the spotlight on the little-known funeral industry—that was all the fox's doing—but I was determined not to let it go out. It was a thrill to watch the community of followers on my Instagram account @la_vie_au_cimetiere grow. Through photographs, I could show the world that on the other side of the gates, there is much more than death: passionate women and men work in the shadows, and glorious nature is reclaiming its rights.

When I was offered the opportunity to share my experience with readers, I jumped at the chance. Père-Lachaise has already been the subject of countless books, but despite its international renown, I find that most people still have a distorted vision of the cemetery, one based on preconceived notions and fantasies of all kinds. In this book, I will do my utmost to lift the curtain on its mysteries.

Beyond the gates of Père-Lachaise, between the gravestones and verdant walkways, lies an entire world I hope to introduce to my readers. I want to provide access to this unknown universe, a place too often ill regarded and feared whose purpose is nonetheless to ease sorrows. May you smile, wonder, marvel, and perhaps even find a little comfort in these pages.

16, Rue du Repos

THE FIRST TIME I sat down at my desk on the ground floor of the administrative offices at Père-Lachaise Cemetery, one thing immediately struck me: since the building had been built on a slope, my office window was so high on the wall that I had look up to see the outside world. It was very unsettling at first. From their vantage point on the Avenue du Puits, curious passersby liked to observe me from above. Sometimes I even heard them thinking aloud: "Hey, do people actually work here?" As if the idea were absurd. The boldest among them had no problem tapping on the glass to ask for a map or directions to the nearest restroom. Once, a little boy I guessed to be around five grabbed the security bars and made faces at me through the window while his father made a phone call. That was the last straw! I decided to put up one-way-mirror film to protect myself from nosy pedestrians, and I've never looked back. The magic screen keeps me from feeling like an animal in a cage—even if people do occasionally use my window to fix their hair or adjust their tie, never imagining that on the other side, someone is doing their job... six feet under.

◇◇◇◇

THOUGH THE DECOR of my new workspace was rather unremarkable, it did feature two unique pieces. The first was a bust of Jim Morrison that sat in the wall niche opposite my desk. Even in my own office, I couldn't escape the cemetery's most famous occupant. The bust was first placed on the singer's grave in the early 1990s, but my predecessor removed it not long after because the cemetery had never received proper authorization from the family. Now it sat before me, waiting for its sculptor to come reclaim it. The bust isn't what you'd call a masterpiece. In fact, it doesn't even look much like Jim Morrison. It looks more like Val Kilmer, the actor who played him in the Oliver Stone movie *The Doors*. Nevertheless, it accompanied me through those early years, lending a rock 'n' roll vibe to my austere office. But it was no match for the portrait of Morrison that I received from street artist Christian Guémy, a.k.a. C215. Stenciled onto an old "Père Lachaise" Métro sign, the striking likeness made the bust look dated in contrast, and I decided to put it in storage. There was only room for one Jim.

The second piece, which still hangs in my office to this day, is an imposing watercolor of Père-Lachaise as seen from the top of a building on Boulevard de Ménilmontant. The cemetery's main monuments are visible, along with the original crematorium (without the dome). The painting, attributed to a certain Julien Garnier, dates back to around 1889. It has been handed down from one curator to the next for more than a century, like a treasure to safeguard. Chief among its merits is the reminder that we are but passing civil servants, mere mortals in a long line, and that the cemetery will outlast us all.

Apart from the bust and the painting, my office looked like any other. Files were stacked everywhere, piles of unfinished business left by the previous curator. Before I had even opened them, the sheer quantity gave me some idea of the task that lay ahead. There would be many fascinating projects to manage and as many problems to solve.

◇◇◇◇

I WAS APPOINTED curator of Père-Lachaise on August 1, 2018, after spending eight years working at the Ivry Cemetery, just outside Paris. While I felt a sense of pride and had the vague but pleasant sensation that I'd been awarded a rare distinction at only thirty-six years old, the euphoria quickly gave way to anxiety. To be honest, I was scared. The landmark had such history. Would I prove equal to the task? In addition to the imposter syndrome that has often made me doubt my legitimacy, I instantly felt the gravity of this legendary cemetery, today the jewel in the crown of cemetery tourism. From 2006 to 2010, I had done a stint at Père-Lachaise as assistant general counsel for the City of Paris Division of Cemeteries, but my knowledge of the

place was still limited to the broad outlines of its history, famous graves, and a handful of urban legends. I would need to familiarize myself with Père-Lachaise's complexity and richness. I'd have to understand it from all angles if I were to live up to its reputation, act as its worthy representative, and manage it to the best of my ability. With a mixture of fear and excitement, I stepped into my new role.

Who can be interred at Père-Lachaise today?

Père-Lachaise accepts around three thousand new occupants each year. This is possible in part through cremation, which makes the cemetery one of the most sought-after resting places in the city. The ashes of Parisians or people who have died in the city can be sprinkled on the lawn of Division 77, commonly known as the Memorial Garden. The crematorium—the only one in Paris—performs an average of six thousand cremations a year.

Families who do not wish to scatter the ashes of a loved one can purchase a niche in the columbarium to house the urn, providing the deceased resided in Paris at the time of death. With 26,600 niches spread across four exterior wings, one crypt, and two vast lower levels, the columbarium has ample capacity.

And then there are all the people, Parisians or not, who already have a family plot in the cemetery. The seventy thousand tombs, acquired in some cases several generations ago,

16, RUE DU REPOS

WHILE ITS OFFICIAL address translates to "16 Street of Rest," there is nothing restful about managing Père-Lachaise. From my earliest days on the job, I was sucked into a whirlwind of activity. Père-Lachaise is neither a necropolis frozen in time nor an open-air museum designed for mass tourism. More than two hundred years after opening its doors, the cemetery is still incredibly busy. Burial plots are sold, and others belong to beneficiaries both in France and abroad. People come from all over the world to be buried at Père-Lachaise in the plot inherited from a distant ancestor. With memorial ceremonies spread over four different spaces, the cemetery handles approximately twenty-three hearses per working day.

Père-Lachaise's average annual statistics (2018–2021):
- 1,000 burials
- 550 columbarium interments
- 1,300 ash scatterings
- 725 concessions either issued or renewed
- 130 exhumations at the request of families
- 400 exhumations for administrative purposes
- 6,000 cremations
- 1,600 work orders to graves (maintenance, engraving, erecting monuments)
- 150 commemorative ceremonies

are recycled. Cracked, crumbling, moss-covered tombs disappear, and fresher, cleaner headstones appear in their place. New epitaphs are engraved while others fade over time. Coffins are brought into the crematorium and leave as urns. Some remains are transferred to the ossuary, and others are interred in a freshly poured burial vault. It is this flurry of activity that keeps the heart of Père-Lachaise beating.

◇◇◇◇◇

IN ORDER FOR Père-Lachaise to preserve its influence and appeal, I believe it's important for the cemetery to continue serving its primary function—that is, burying the dead. To do this, it must constantly adapt to the times, to changing customs, language, style, and methods. Père-Lachaise responds to shifts in society; instead of remaining impervious to the outside world, it must meet the ever-changing funerary needs of the living to help them with the grieving process. Over the centuries, Père-Lachaise has been remade countless times. This ability to continually reinvent itself breathes new life and soul into its walls while preserving its very essence.

Take the influence of religion, for example. As its role in society has waned over time, so has its place in the cemetery. While faith-based sections dedicated to Jews and Muslims can still be visited for historical purposes, they have long since ceased to be in use. Today, no distinction is made between religious and nonreligious occupants, reflecting the diversity of our society. Although the East Chapel—reserved for Catholic funerals—is still in use, it is a legacy of the past whose activity is now marginal.

In another sign of changing customs, the facilities dedicated to cremation—the crematorium, columbarium, and Memorial Garden—currently make up the largest part of the cemetery's activity. To keep up with growing demand for cremation while preserving nineteenth-century funerary heritage, the administration has been restoring and repurposing abandoned chapels by transforming them into columbaria. Like the ouroboros, the symbol of the serpent eating its own tail that figures on a great many tombs, everything is constantly being reborn.

◇◇◇◇◇

DESPITE WHAT SOME may think, being the curator of Père-Lachaise is about so much more than arranging the occasional celebrity burial. I am not a heritage manager (I'm not an expert in art or science), and I don't have encyclopedic knowledge of the bodies buried here (many historians, tour guides, and enthusiasts know far more than I do). I am not a curate either (though some of the residents of Père-Lachaise may have been), and I have little knowledge of curatives (though I do keep a box of bandages in my office). Being curator of Père-Lachaise is about rubbing shoulders with death, with the departed of all stripes, and with the loved ones they leave behind. I spend my days talking about coffins, ashes, vaults, remains transfers, exhumations, burial rights, and tombstones. I oversee funeral processions and commemorative ceremonies. I run an establishment whose users have one thing in common: they're all sad. I have a job some find scary but which I consider to be one of the most beautiful acts of public service. I'm not saying this because I have an unhealthy or morbid attraction to the profession. I am not obsessed with death. In fact, I scarcely see it.

Managing a cemetery is first and foremost about accompanying the living.

Tombstone Tourism

"Père-lachaise is the Disneyland of graveyards!" Behind this amusing comparison I once heard lies a perception held by many tourists—one that isn't entirely false.

The main attractions, of course, are the celebrity tombs that draw throngs of sightseers. Just like at an amusement park, visitors have to wait in line on the busiest days to see the graves of Frédéric Chopin, Jim Morrison, or Édith Piaf. They are taken back in time by professional guides who chronicle the lives of the cemetery's most illustrious occupants. As each tragedy or comedy unfolds, tourists embark—willingly or not—on an emotional roller coaster. The most sensitive may find that the experience renders their own mortality far too tangible. Everyone feels slightly disoriented amid the tombs of the rich and famous, struck by the decor around them: statues, epitaphs, busts, splashes of the macabre, funerary symbolism, and even necrophagous trees that grow unbidden up through the graves themselves, splitting the stones and consuming the iron fencing. The natural entwinement of vegetable and mineral creates a striking poetry.

Some visitors, dizzy at the sight of tombs stretching in all directions, feel the memories of loved ones resurface. Others are sickened by the Holocaust memorials that remind them what evil can accomplish. Thrill-seekers get all the goosebumps they need thanks to the cemetery's countless myths and legends. As families make their way out through the Porte du Repos, they'll snap a selfie in front of the Adam family grave and post it to social media, along with the obligatory skull-and-crossbones emoji. Like at an amusement park, visitors won't be able to see the entire cemetery in a single day—just ask their feet.

Today, Père-Lachaise is a hotspot for tourism and culture that attracts approximately three million visitors a year. Tourists of all kinds consider the cemetery one of Paris's biggest attractions. Tour operators include visits to Père-Lachaise in their packages alongside other iconic sites, such as the Louvre, Montmartre, and the Eiffel Tower. One major perk is that the famed and fascinating burial grounds are free to enter.

◇◇◇◇◇

FROM MY FIRST days on the job, I came to realize that Père-Lachaise is indeed an unusual place. I was struck in particular by the mix of people who found themselves inside its offices: grieving families inquiring about their concession often rub shoulders with tourists in shorts looking for a map to locate the graves of Marcel Proust or Maria Callas. Outside the offices, it's no different: groups of visitors dressed in bright summer outfits wander between funeral processions of families dressed all in black. The one thing they have in common? Sunglasses. This diversity is a key feature of Père-Lachaise; it makes it a cosmopolitan and singular place, though constant vigilance is required to ensure both groups can coexist without incident.

It's difficult to pinpoint exactly when tombstone tourism began. As early as 1808, Antoine Caillot published *A Picturesque and Sentimental Trip to the Resting Field Under Montmartre, and to Father Lachaise's Country House in Montlouis.* It would be the first guidebook in a long series. In addition to listing the graves and their epitaphs, Caillot describes the atmosphere of the cemetery and shares his own reflections inspired by a visit. Four years after opening its doors, Père-Lachaise was already kindling a certain fascination—a telltale sign of the tourist attraction it would become over the course of the nineteenth century.

Less than fifty years later, in 1855, F. T. Salomon published *An Alphabetical Guide to Perpetual Concessions*, in which he writes that "the foreigner to Paris will visit Père-Lachaise, this necropolis that, owing to its sites and overall quality, has become the subject of universal admiration. If he loves art, he will find treasures crafted by the masters themselves; if he loves history, he will behold the histories

of great men." Salomon notes that Père-Lachaise is filled "daily with crowds of people from all countries, all nations, come to visit the mortal remains of celebrities laid to rest, to admire the art which seems to hail from all corners of the world or to pay homage to a relative, friend, etc."

Nearly two hundred years on, this observation still rings true. Thanks to an ever-growing list of celebrities interred within its walls, Père-Lachaise has become a second Pantheon, housing great talents of all kinds and from all eras. It is the final resting place of actors, painters, architects, photographers, singers, filmmakers, scientists, writers, poets, historians, military men and women, and leaders, in addition to many foreign notables who left their homelands and found refuge in France for historical or political reasons. Their presence adds an international dimension to the cemetery. Americans make pilgrimages to the graves of Jim Morrison and Gertrude Stein; Poles honor the memory of Frédéric Chopin; Kurds pay their respects to singer Ahmet Kaya and filmmaker Yilmaz Güney; Italians visit the graves of Luigi Cherubini and Amedeo Modigliani; the Irish and the English are drawn to the emasculated sphinx on Oscar Wilde's tomb; Armenians kneel before the cenotaph to General Antranik Ozanian; Belgians flock to the dramatic sculpture that sits atop the tomb of writer Georges Rodenbach; and Brazilians come to place a hand on the bust of Allan Kardec, founder of Spiritism, who, though French, is incredibly popular in Brazil.

This open-air Who's Who practically overshadows the site's primary function, to the point that many visitors expect a museum-like welcome including guided tours, audio guides, lockers, and a cafeteria. They are astonished to discover that Père-Lachaise is a working cemetery, complete with hearses and sad people. Worse still, there is no train ride or luggage storage, so the little wheels of their suitcases have to contend with two-hundred-year-old cobblestones. Left to their own devices, many end up with their noses in their phones, desperately trying to find the famous graves they came to see.

The best-prepared tourists will have hired a flesh-and-blood guide. These guides operate independently and offer tours on a wide range of themes as diverse as Père-Lachaise's residents. Whether they are self-taught or licensed tour guides, most have an outgoing personality suited to the theatrical nature of the job. Egos do sometimes get in the way, causing conflict, resentment, finger-pointing, and accusations of plagiarism. A word of advice: avoid the guides who stand inside the cemetery trying loudly and insistently to drum up business. Not only is this prohibited, but they are usually the least skilled.

Whatever their background or personality, the guides deserve credit for bringing memory to life and doing their best to make a stroll among the dead a pleasant experience, sometimes in difficult weather conditions. Tourists will spend two or three hours learning fascinating tidbits of trivia and listening to countless anecdotes. Afterward, they may have a sudden urge to listen to The Doors, reread Proust, or visit the Louvre to check out a Delacroix or two. And yet, while they've satisfied their thirst for culture, they haven't really discovered the true Père-Lachaise. They'll leave knowing more about its dead residents than about the cemetery itself.

My friends and family regularly ask me to accompany them through the cemetery. They're afraid of getting lost or of not being able to find the graves they want to see. I tell them that the beauty of Père-Lachaise lies in the fact that you can easily get lost. What I love most about the cemetery isn't the celebrity graves but the bewitching sensation you can only truly experience when you're no longer sure of where you are.

Can you bring children to a cemetery?

Absolutely! Naturally, you'll need to have a conversation about death with your children, but you won't traumatize them. They'll be curious and will ask questions that might surprise you. "When you die, is it for life?" my daughter once asked me. You may not always have a ready answer. You'll begin a conversation, try out certain metaphors, and search for words. But you mustn't lie or hide the truth; leaving your children alone with their fears and anxieties would be much worse.

Visiting a cemetery with your children is the perfect opportunity to have your first discussions on the meaning of life. "Why do we die?" "Where do we go when we're dead?" "Does dying hurt?" "Do you want to be cremated or buried?" I believe that answering their questions and confronting the

This is the reason I generally recommend visiting or revisiting Père-Lachaise without a guide, armed only with a paper map and the goal of seeing no more than a dozen tombs. You're guaranteed to lose your way in the vast network of paths, go around in circles, and return to the same place several times before you end up asking for directions. You'll struggle to read the map, perhaps even squabble with your partner ("I told you we were supposed to turn right!"), and always remember the time you argued in the middle of the cemetery. You'll wander into hidden corners, stumble upon poignant epitaphs, admire the poetry of certain taboos will help them accept death, which is a part of their lives whether you like it or not.

You'll also help your children develop other skill sets. They'll hone their sense of direction, learn to read a map, practice sounding out epitaphs or decoding Roman numerals, calculate the age at which a person died, observe the birds and trees, and gather chestnuts. When they find themselves face-to-face with a child's grave, they'll realize that death affects everyone, not just Grandma and Grandpa, which is why their parents always remind them to look both ways before crossing the street. Talking about death with your children will help them get more out of life. So, take them to Père-Lachaise—they'll thank you for it later.

areas, stroll along the picturesque Chemin des Chèvres, linger over the grave of a stranger, or marvel at the elaborate tombstones built to honor past luminaries. You'll feel as though you've stepped out of time, out of Paris, and into another place entirely. You might not have found the graves you were looking for, but you'll have found the real Père-Lachaise—you'll feel it in your bones—and walk away with a lasting impression. To my mind, this is the true Père-Lachaise experience. It will take your breath away and spark an irrepressible desire to come back, just so you can lose yourself in it all over again.

◇◇◇◇◇

GIVEN THE LARGE crowds, security is a daily concern of mine. I work to ensure that visitors' peace of mind isn't disturbed by rude encounters or pickpockets. Since the cemetery's security guards are primarily tasked with overseeing funeral operations, troops deployed under the antiterrorist force Opération Sentinelle carry out daily security patrols. The National Police and the cavalry regiment of the Republican Guard also make regular rounds. Although visitors rarely feel at risk due to the cemetery's tranquil atmosphere, Père-Lachaise is nonetheless one of the most closely monitored sites in eastern Paris for several reasons: it sees a high volume of foot traffic, it is a memorial site featuring numerous commemorative monuments, it carries out nearly ten thousand funeral operations a year, and it houses France's largest crematorium as well as a Catholic chapel that performs blessings and funeral rites for the deceased.

One of the most challenging tasks is to clear out the cemetery each night. Security guards ring a bell fifteen minutes before closing, signaling to visitors that they should make their way toward an exit. If only this were enough! Between the tourists who are in no hurry to leave, those who won't leave until they've seen one last grave, those who can't find their way out, and those who get locked in (voluntarily or not), closing the gates is a team effort that requires vigilance and coordination to ensure that everyone makes it out on time—which rarely happens.

When visitors fail to leave on time and find themselves locked in the cemetery, some bang on the office door in a panic, hoping a kind soul working late will let them out. Others call the police and plead to have a cemetery employee sent over as quickly as possible to open the gates. A few hear my children through an open window of our apartment and cry out in desperation, "Is anyone there?!" I always take pity on them and go downstairs to open the gate, asking the same question every time: "Didn't you hear the closing bell?" Some people are sincere in their apologies. "We're so sorry, we didn't hear a thing! We've spent the past hour wandering around, completely lost. The place is deserted, and we were terrified we'd have to spend the night here..." Others are less sincere and clearly ignored the closing bell on purpose. Some even have the gall to blame me. "What do you mean, six PM? That's so early for a tourist attraction! You could be more accommodating."

THE PAST FEW years have seen a rise in a new type of tourism aimed at making Père-Lachaise more fun to visit. Several companies have organized treasure hunts and escape games within the cemetery walls. This type of entertainment is inappropriate for such a setting and is strictly prohibited. Grieving families shouldn't be disturbed by victory-hungry participants running or shouting along the paths. Theatrical or musical performances are occasionally permitted, such as for the Printemps des cimetières, a national event celebrating France's funerary heritage, but these exceptions are strictly regulated.

Though Père-Lachaise is an undeniable tourist attraction, it's not an amusement park. Regardless of what people think, it's still a cemetery. Ironically, Disney's administration recently had to remind guests that its amusement parks weren't... cemeteries! Particularly in the United States, where visitors have taken to spreading the ashes of loved ones near their favorite rides. To each their own problems.

Life at the Cemetery

MY FIRST EXPERIENCE as a cemetery curator was at the Ivry Cemetery, just outside Paris. When I stepped into the role in 2010, I'd never been handed so much autonomy or responsibility. After taking some time to settle in, I gradually modified a number of internal procedures and set out to improve archive conservation. In truth, this is a curator's raison d'être: it fell to me to "curate" the cemetery's archives, and I didn't do things by halves. My team and I digitized all records and overhauled the system for organizing concessions. It was nothing exciting, but I wanted to do right by my cemetery and manage it to the best of my ability.

Looking back on this period, I realize that despite having seventy acres at my disposal, I spent most of my time in my office and only ventured outside when it was absolutely necessary. I never took advantage of the natural beauty around me. Worse still, I scarcely took the time to become acquainted with the site's features. I focused only on funerary logistics: managing burials, overseeing procedure, and supporting bereaved families.

To me, the cemetery's natural elements were just a managerial headache. While its 1,900 trees were no doubt beautiful, all I saw were the piles of leaves the groundskeepers would have to rake and the complaints that might land on my desk as a result. And although I noticed the cemetery was home to a wide variety of birds, including what looked like parrots, I was primarily concerned with the droppings that littered the benches and tombstones. In those days, biodiversity was the least of my worries, and my environmental awareness was limited to recycling.

◇◇◇◇

IN 2011, Paris City Council passed a biodiversity plan calling on Parisian cemeteries to reduce their pesticide use. For decades, maintenance crews had sprayed walkways with weed killer whose stated goal was to destroy any wild plant that had the audacity to grow between gravestones. Each spring, the weeks-long crusade required workers to show up in full-body protective gear, and the treated sections had to be temporarily closed to the public. Only after the green areas had been sprayed with chemicals would they be deemed "clean," i.e., lifeless. The result met user expectations and matched my own understanding of cemeteries, namely that everything surrounding the deceased should be dead, like them. Any trace of life was seen as a sign of disrespect. Flowers were allowed, but only if they were in planters. Even then, most were only used once a year, on All Saints' Day, for the traditional chrysanthemums. Flowers had their place—as long as that place was on the headstones.

◇◇◇◇◇

NATURALLY, THE CEMETERY'S grand avenues were lined with majestic trees and shrub beds. Greenery was not, however, encouraged to flourish inside the confines of its forty-seven divisions. Only one was designated as "landscaped," meaning that a few trees and shrubs had been planted between the graves. But this division was considered the experimental work of a long-gone landscape engineer. It represented an acceptable level of disorder within a cemetery whose rows of graves were aligned with military precision. In other words, it was the touch of whimsy that proved we were open-minded and not overly rigid.

When it came time to enforce the new pesticide-free policy, my knee-jerk reaction was "Why are we doing this? We'll be swamped with complaints. We're a cemetery, not a park!" You could say I was hostile to the idea. But my teams and I didn't have a say in the matter, so we played along to placate our superiors and elected representatives. At their request, no chemicals would be used in three of the cemetery's designated pesticide-free divisions. We didn't realize it then, but a small revolution was taking root.

THE TRANSFORMATION PROCESS took four years, during which time my attitude and that of my colleagues changed radically. As the years passed, more divisions were designated as pesticide-free. We received help from a consulting agency, purchased machinery and other equipment, trained groundskeepers in new maintenance techniques, seeded divisions that proved difficult to regreen, and brought in a landscaping company to gradually grass over the sidewalks. Meanwhile, cemetery staff were so inspired that at the end of 2014, we made the decision to stop using pesticides across the entire seventy-acre site.

What could explain such a radical shift? It was the green. The power of green. It goes without saying that green paths are prettier than dirt or gravel paths. Once we surrendered our chemicals, the cemetery began to change before our eyes, becoming an oasis of foliage bursting with natural beauty. The groundskeepers, whose work had always been considerably undervalued, also experienced a shift in their role. Up to that point, they had toiled thanklessly in the shadows. Nobody gave them a second thought unless there was a problem: if there were piles of leaves, dirty toilets, or overflowing trash cans, the groundskeepers weren't doing their jobs. The pesticide-free policy thrust these workers into the limelight by giving them a chance to play up the site's aesthetics. They gained visibility by trading in their weed killer for lawn mowers. Visitors began to admire the grounds in the wake of their efforts, and the groundskeepers started to take pride in their work. In the end, those four years taught us a beautiful lesson: how to balance respect for the dead with respect for life.

◇◇◇◇◇

ON A PERSONAL level, I credit the zero-pesticide policy with opening my eyes to the cemetery I managed. As the paths greened over, so did my attitude. I became fascinated by the rainbow of wildflowers: the deep-blue grape hyacinths, the bright-yellow lotus, the orange marigolds, and the lizard orchids that smelled strongly of goats. The cemetery began to feel more like the countryside, and I was increasingly aware of how lucky I was to exist inside this bubble of biodiversity wedged between the high-rises of the Parisian suburbs. As wildflowers proliferated, they attracted butterflies, bees, and other insects. A new ecosystem was emerging.

And yet, I lacked the knowledge to fully appreciate the transformation unfolding before my eyes. My field of expertise is the funeral industry; I didn't know much about plants and animals. It was a chance encounter with Pierre, one of the cemetery's regular birdwatchers who lived nearby, that changed my outlook forever. Our paths crossed one afternoon, and the amateur ornithologist took the time to explain his observations and what they meant for the area's biodiversity. It dawned on me that the cemetery was home to an exceptional array of wildlife, and I wanted to learn more. From then on, whenever I walked the grounds, I would look beyond the gravestones to watch the titmice, starlings, blackbirds, rose-ringed parakeets, woodpeckers, and other birds flitting from tree to tree.

⬦⬦⬦

IN 2015, WE stopped using pesticides altogether. By fate or by coincidence, that was the same year my wife and I got married. Before we left for our honeymoon, we bought a DSLR camera to document the trip. After we'd returned from Thailand, I thought it would be a shame to leave the camera in the closet, so I decided to bring it with me on my walks around the cemetery to refine my technique. Little by little, I weaned myself off the automatic setting and began manually photographing the scenes I wanted to capture. In so doing, I started to observe the cemetery with a different eye—that of the photographer. Everything changes when you look at the world through a camera lens: taking the perfect shot means constantly being on the lookout for the right aesthetics, composition, emotion, or je ne sais quoi; you have to be fully in the moment. Headstone details, kitschy family plaques, epitaphs with spelling errors, even autumn-tinged landscapes—I saw everything through new eyes. Over time, I tried to document the cemetery's animals, insects, birds, and, of course, its cats. Photographing wildlife is no easy task; it requires patience, anticipation, and quick reflexes—all qualities I would need to develop.

⬦⬦⬦

IN 2017, TO my great surprise, we were joined by a new group of playmates. After six years of transformation to promote biodiversity, a family of foxes took up residence in Ivry Cemetery. You can imagine our pride! We took their arrival as the reward for our efforts to make the cemetery a place not only for the dead but also for life. Suddenly, I found myself photographing foxes and their kits, hedgehogs, squirrels, and even tawny owls in my own backyard. I could scarcely believe it; although I'd grown up in the countryside, I was seeing more wild animals in the city than I ever had before. My pictures of wildlife began to pile up, and I found it hard to keep my newfound treasures to myself. I wanted to share them with other people and shed light on this aspect of the cemetery. If my own attitude had changed, so could others'. My wife always gives excellent advice, and one day she floated the idea of taking to social media. "You should open an Instagram account," she told me.

On June 3, 2017, @la_vie_au_cimetiere was born.

◇◇◇◇◇

IN EARLY 2018, I learned that my colleague and fellow curator at the Montparnasse Cemetery had decided to retire. After spending eight years at Ivry, I felt ready to move on. I was itching to manage a cemetery within the city limits, one that presented the additional challenges of being a heritage and tourist site. Managing Montparnasse also meant managing its satellite cemeteries, including Passy, which may have the highest ratio of famous residents per square foot in the city. I applied for the job, hoping I'd get it. Unfortunately, my boss called in early April to tell me another of my colleagues had been chosen. "It's a shame, but..." He went on to say that the curator of Père-Lachaise was planning to retire around the same time and that he wanted me to apply for the job.

"Really?" I marveled.

I'm frequently asked how one becomes curator of Père-Lachaise. I always reply, "By accident." And yet, deep down, I've often wondered if it was my destiny. I've never believed that our fate is written in the stars; a life without surprises would be too sad. But I have to admit that, looking back, it does seem like an invisible hand gave me a nudge—two nudges, really—in the right direction.

The Flagship

AFTER HANDING OFF the daily operations at Ivry, I took up the reins at Père-Lachaise. As I stepped into my new role, a colleague remarked that I'd traded the helm of a frigate to captain the flagship. It seemed an apt comparison. It's no secret that Père-Lachaise is the most legendary necropolis in the world, the global standard of resting places. People from all over have heard of it, and it's frequently referenced in the French press to describe different cemeteries (e.g., "the London equivalent of Père-Lachaise," "the Père-Lachaise of Naples"). These labels make it seem as if Père-Lachaise has left a trail of offspring all over the world. Pretty ironic for a cemetery that's named after a priest!

In France, Père-Lachaise is held so high in public regard that its name is almost synonymous with cemeteries themselves. This is clear to me every day as I sift through the requests we receive. Many people write to find out where an ancestor's tomb is located, believing—incorrectly—that we maintain the archives for every cemetery in France. We frequently receive calls from civil servants with very specific questions about concession law, hoping that our industry knowledge extends to their situation. We also receive requests from foreign cemetery directors and diplomats who want to see first-hand how Père-Lachaise is managed as both a tourist destination and heritage site. I once met with a delegation from South Korea who were doing research for a cemetery they hoped to build near Seoul. Another time, I gave a cemetery tour to a foreign dignitary who was on an official visit to France.

While Père-Lachaise has become the ultimate cultural touchstone, its early days weren't without their challenges.

⋄⋄⋄⋄

BEFORE PÈRE-LACHAISE OPENED in 1804, the overwhelming majority of Parisians were buried in common graves scattered across the city's parish cemeteries. No need for a coffin or individual burial plot; bodies were simply piled on top of one another, separated only by a layer of dirt, in open pits in churchyards. What mattered most was to be interred in consecrated ground and be given a Christian burial. At that time, cemeteries weren't open spaces where grieving families could come to honor the memory of their loved ones. They were restricted places that denied funeral rites to anyone who had been excommunicated from the Church. The insalubrious nature of these macabre millefeuilles led to major public health issues. Over the course of the eighteenth century, advances in medical knowledge and a fear of epidemics stoked criticism of these fetid cesspools of disease that were so near to residential areas. In 1765, the Parlement of Paris issued a ruling that banned cemeteries within city limits and transferred them to sites outside the capital. For reasons mainly related to high costs and force of habit, the ban met with strong opposition and was never enforced. Religious authorities who managed the common graves failed to create new burial grounds outside Paris, and bodies continued piling up in their cemeteries. As is often the case, a scandal had to erupt to effect lasting change.

◇◇◇◇◇

FOR CENTURIES, the Holy Innocents' Cemetery was the largest burial ground in Paris. This patch of land measuring just over two acres wasn't a cemetery in the way we think of today. Named for the associated church of Les Innocents, the site featured a common grave and several charnel houses. From the twelfth to the eighteenth century, it served as the resting place for generations of Parisians. The complex sat in the heart of Paris, in the Les Halles district, under what is now Place Joachim-du-Bellay. On May 7, 1780, an underground ossuary collapsed, spilling the mephitic remains of rotting corpses into the cellars of neighboring homes. The public outcry was swift, prompting the Parlement of Paris to enact new legislation that banned inhumations at the Holy Innocents beginning November 1. Between 1785 and 1787, bones were exhumed and transported from the Holy Innocents to a massive ossuary now famously known as the Paris Catacombs.

Though the threat to public health had been mitigated at the Holy Innocents, it would take years before Paris officially

banned the existence of other common graves. Twenty-four years later, Napoleon I issued his Imperial Decree of 23 Prairial year XII (June 12, 1804), codifying the present-day system of burial practices in France. The decree established a strict separation between spaces for the living and the dead: cemeteries were required to be outside city limits, "at least thirty-five to forty meters from their borders." It also reinforced secularization, a process that had begun under the French Revolution, by transferring burial responsibilities from the clergy to municipal authorities. All cities and towns had to comply with this new, more hygienic form of burial, as laid out in article 3 of the decree: "Select the most elevated sites, preferably those with northern exposure; they will be enclosed by a wall at least two meters in height. The land should be well planted, taking the proper precautions so as not to interfere with air circulation." Common graves were explicitly forbidden, and the dead were to be buried in individual plots "separated by a distance of thirty to forty centimeters on either side, and thirty to fifty centimeters from the head and feet." In short, new cemeteries broke with the traditions of the pre-revolution Ancien Régime.

⋄⋄⋄⋄⋄

ON MAY 21, 1804, less than a month before the new decree was issued, the Cemetery of the East officially opened its doors, despite being woefully incomplete. Located outside the Paris city limits, the cemetery that would come to be known as Père-Lachaise was the first in France to meet the new regulations established under Napoleon I.

Alexandre-Théodore Brongniart, an architect best known today for designing the Paris stock exchange building, was commissioned by prefect Nicolas Frochot to design the new cemetery. Brongniart wanted to preserve the site's natural landscape, which had previously been a Jesuit retreat and home to Father François d'Aix de La Chaize, confessor to King Louis XIV. Although he kept some of the site's winding paths, wooded areas, and other vegetation, Brongniart widened certain walkways to create large boulevards that he lined with trees to distinguish areas meant for foot traffic from those reserved for burial plots. He adapted his design to the natural features of the land, which cut through the Charonne hillside, by laying steps and building low walls for support.

In addition to landscaping that was revolutionary for its time, Brongniart had planned to erect several architectural landmarks within the vast, rugged grounds: an imposing semicircular entrance, three circular green spaces reserved for monuments, a chapel for funeral processions, and a great pyramid that would house funeral ceremonies of all faiths. Brongniart's designs laid the foundation for a new type of cemetery landscape. Inspired by English-style gardens, his sprawling necropolis replaced the traditional parish cemetery and its common graves. Père-Lachaise quickly became a model for cemeteries across France and around the world.

◇◇◇◇◇

BRONGNIART DIED IN 1813, before he could see many of his expansive projects to completion. His successors would draw inspiration from his work and respect his original intentions. The monumental main gate, which was designed by Étienne-Hippolyte Godde and finished in 1821, is very similar to Brongniart's own design. In 1823, Godde also constructed a rather ordinary neoclassical chapel to replace the pyramid of Brongniart's imagination. Pity—to think Père-Lachaise could have boasted a pyramid even before the Louvre! It's nonetheless heartening to learn the chapel was built using stones from its namesake's former home, and its forecourt offers a breathtaking view of Paris—including the Pantheon, Père-Lachaise's biggest rival. It is also the place where Rastignac uttered his famous line, "It's war between us now!" in the final scene of *Père Goriot* by Balzac, who is himself buried a stone's throw away (Division 48).[1] Although Brongniart's monuments never saw the light of day, two of the sites reserved for them are now home to the majestic tombs of statesman Casimir Perier (1832) and diplomat Félix de Beaujour (1836).

⋄⋄⋄⋄⋄

IT TOOK MANY YEARS for Père-Lachaise to become the cemetery we know today. Parisians continued to bury their dead in common graves for some time, despite the practice being outlawed under the 1804 decree. Père-Lachaise's own records confirm that common graves were in use through 1873. They were originally located in the lower and slightly sloped part of the cemetery along Boulevard de Ménilmontant, at one time the site of a vegetable garden. After the necropolis was enlarged, the common graves were scattered across other divisions, in particular those located on what's known today as the plateau. The cemetery didn't record the names of people buried in common graves prior to 1818, so the identity of the first person to be buried at Père-Lachaise in this manner remains a mystery.

The 1804 decree introduced a new system of individual burial meant to supplant the common graves. There were two options under this system: a free temporary plot, which was available to the public but would be recycled after five years; or the much more exclusive paid concession, which could be either temporary or permanent. Cemetery records tell us that a five-year-old girl named Adélaïde Paillard de Villeneuve was the first person to be buried in an individual grave, on June 4, 1804. Because it was issued as a five-year plot, her grave marker was removed and has been lost to history. The headstone of Reine Févez, the second person to be buried in a temporary individual grave, on June 18, 1804, can be found in Division 60 along the circular avenue. Although her tomb was relocated from its initial resting place, it's still the oldest grave in the cemetery.

The exclusive paid type of burial, known as a concession, was only granted to those who "established foundations or made donations to benefit hospitals or the poor, in addition to a sum to be given to the municipality" and who "wish[ed] to possess a distinct and separate plot for their grave and the graves of their relatives or descendants on which to erect monuments or tombstones."[2] Only the wealthiest Parisians were able to afford this type of burial. Concessions were reserved for the hilly wooded part of the cemetery that resembled an English garden, known today as the romantic sector. The first concession was granted on July 9, 1804, to Pierre Jacquemart, a founder of one of the earliest banks in Paris. His grave, which is still maintained by his descendants, is located in Division 29. It is likely the oldest burial concession in France as defined by the 1804 decree.

◇◇◇◇◇

DESPITE THE NEW LEGISLATION and Brongniart's radical landscape designs, the Cemetery of the East was unpopular among Parisians. The public wasn't used to having a relationship with death—or rather, with the dead. In addition, bodies had to be transported farther afield to a poor, working-class neighborhood outside the city lines. Visiting the dead, a fairly new concept in itself, suddenly required advance planning. In its early days, the cemetery was intended to serve a largely hygienic purpose: each day, some twenty-five bodies from the city were interred in its common graves. Very few Parisians were able to benefit from the new regulations and erect a tombstone—often a very modest one—to honor their dead. Individual concessions were rare and exceptional privileges. It wasn't until 1817 that things began to change.

In December 1816, the French government decided to close the Museum of French Monuments, an art museum founded by archaeologist Alexandre Lenoir, and reassign its buildings to the School of Fine Arts. The museum housed the tombs of several celebrities, which needed an immediate transfer elsewhere. Père-Lachaise was deemed the ideal resting place for these illustrious figures, and the remains of Molière and La Fontaine were officially interred there on March 6, 1817. Today, monuments commemorating the playwright and fabulist can be found in the same enclosure.

The remains of star-crossed lovers Abelard and Heloise were also transferred to Père-Lachaise in 1817. The legendary

How do we know they are the actual remains of Molière and La Fontaine?

We don't—in fact, they most likely aren't. Molière was buried the night of February 21, 1673, in Saint-Joseph Cemetery, and La Fontaine was buried on April 14, 1695, in the Holy Innocents' Cemetery. On July 6, 1792, two corpses were exhumed from Saint-Joseph and transferred to the Museum of French Monuments. Since La Fontaine wasn't buried in that cemetery, his grave today contains the remains of an unknown corpse. As for Molière, his remains were disinterred from a part of the cemetery where his corpse had supposedly been transferred a few days after his burial. It's very unlikely that Père-Lachaise is his final resting place, especially since some of the corpses buried in the Saint-Joseph Cemetery had begun to be transferred to the Catacombs as early as 1787, prior to its closure in 1796. History would suggest that the *presumed* remains of Molière are lying in rest in Père-Lachaise. Regardless of whether the tombs hold the true remains of either genius, their graves are some of the most visited in the cemetery, honoring their memory and their masterpieces.

pair was laid to rest inside a magnificent chapel, where a sculpture of them lying side by side is visible through the neo-Gothic arcades. They are the cemetery's oldest residents, having died in 1142 and 1164 respectively. The bones of the couple were reinterred several times prior to arriving at Père-Lachaise, but the transfers were so well documented that there is no real doubt as to their authenticity. Like the graves of Molière and La Fontaine, the chapel that houses Abelard and Heloise was classified as a historical monument in 1983.

Though the transfer of these celebrities to Père-Lachaise was in truth a rather unexpected gain following the closure of the Museum of French Monuments, it's often described as a brilliant marketing campaign. Either way, once Parisians got wind of the news, it changed their perception of the cemetery considerably. That same year, Père-Lachaise welcomed several other illustrious residents, including composer Étienne Méhul and military commander André Masséna. The following year, Pierre Beaumarchais, who had been buried in 1799 in his own courtyard along the boulevard that would eventually bear his name, was also transferred to Père-Lachaise after his property was purchased by the City of Paris. Suddenly, Parisians were clamoring to buy a burial concession so they and their loved ones could be laid to rest alongside some of the greatest names in French history. To meet growing demand, Père-Lachaise was expanded five times, most recently in 1850. Today, it covers nearly 110 acres—about the size of Vatican City.

You could say that makes me the Pope of cemeteries, but that's a leap I'm not willing to take.

The Funeral Bug

"How can you work in such a gloomy place? It must be awful!" a person once remarked as I was selling them a burial concession. We were discussing a different matter altogether and the question seemed to come out of nowhere, as if they felt a sudden, overwhelming urge to know why I'd chosen this career path. I felt obliged to justify myself and explain how varied the work is, how I consider myself lucky to work in one of the world's foremost sites for commemorative art. I tried to impress upon them that I mostly deal with the living, of all stripes and from all backgrounds, and that these interactions are the most enriching part of my job—much more so than my proximity to the dead, famous or not.

Apparently, my arguments did nothing to sway their opinion. They declined to take the map and business card I handed them at the end of our meeting, claiming they didn't want to bring them home and "contaminate the house." I didn't take offense; you have to be understanding in the face of grief. I wonder how they would have reacted if I'd told them I live in the cemetery with my family, or that my parents had worked in the industry as well. Because it's true, I was bitten by the funeral bug as a child.

◇◇◇◇

"DID ANYONE DIE TODAY?" It was a question I heard repeated throughout my childhood. Every day, my father would come home from work and ask my mother the same thing. But my father didn't have a morbid obsession with death. He wasn't a detective or a collector of obituaries either. He was a stonemason who ran a funeral monument shop, and death was his business.

For thirty years, my parents managed Gallot Monuments in Bray-sur-Seine, a small town tucked away in a corner of the Île-de-France region. In 1990, they took over the business from my paternal grandparents, who had inherited it from my great-grandfather. It was a family affair, where the personal mixed with the professional all under one roof. Our family lived behind the shop. Same building, same address. A single door separated our living room from the shop where our parents would meet with clients to discuss building a vault or installing a headstone. The desk they used to draw up estimates, phone suppliers, and do the bookkeeping was in our living room, right behind the sofa where we would read or watch TV. The two worlds were fused right down to the phone number, which Gallot Monuments and the Gallot family shared. Whenever my friends called, they were greeted by my mother's voice: "Gallot Monuments, how may we help you?"

Outside, it wasn't much different. The yard I spent so much time playing in with my brother and friends was right next door to the shop's outdoor showroom, which always had at least a dozen headstones on display. I wasn't living in a cemetery yet, but gravestones were already a part of my daily life.

◇◇◇◇

MY PARENTS' ROLE in the funeral business meant that my brother and I were expected to follow certain rules. Under no circumstances was our behavior to disturb the shop's solemnity and professional reputation. The number-one rule was to keep quiet if customers were around, since bereaved families were likely to hear us if we spoke too loudly from the living room. But, like any self-respecting siblings, we liked to argue and fight. Once, I remember our mother had to interrupt a meeting to come separate us, warning us with a fearsome glare to cut it out.

Outside in the yard, the same rules applied: if my parents were walking customers through the showroom to help them choose a monument, we had to go inside. The heaviness of grief, coupled with our parents' professional attitude, spoke for itself. Nobody had to ask us to put our soccer or basketball games on hold—we did it automatically so our yard would reflect the peace and calm of a cemetery.

Choosing a tombstone isn't a pleasant or exciting experience; clients are either buying one for a recently departed loved one or picking out their own. It's always a solemn occasion, and my parents' customers required the utmost serenity to make their choice. "Were you thinking pink granite? Or more of a gray-blue?" The response was often "We want something simple, something understated." In villages, eccentricity is most often frowned upon.

People who were purchasing their own gravestone in advance were in no rush to see it put to use. It was an investment for the future, something they would never enjoy in their lifetime. Some turned to humor to downplay the situation, making comments like "The later the better!" or "We're in no hurry to move to our new 'country house'!"

⋄⋄⋄⋄⋄

"DID ANYONE DIE TODAY?" My father always asked because the answer was likely to affect his work schedule. As deaths were a priority, rush jobs were common. He might have to put a project on hold to build a vault within the six-day window mandated by law. My father was constantly adjusting and reorganizing his employees' schedules to meet deadlines. Death comes unannounced, and burials can't wait.

My father's question also gave my parents an opportunity to say a few words about the deceased, most of whom they'd known. Sooner or later, all two thousand villagers in Bray-sur-Seine would require my parents' services. Gallot Monuments was one of the rare businesses that attracted customers out of necessity rather than desire. As a result, every family knew my mother from the shop and ran into my father when attending burials at the local cemeteries. My parents almost always had something to say about the

recipient of their services. "Mr. Dupont from Mouy? I ran into his wife at Mr. Durand's funeral last week! I had no idea he was so sick." "Mrs. Martin from Mousseaux? She was such a lovely woman! We buried her husband three years ago, remember? Her neighbor told me she never got over it." "Mrs. Blanc's son had a stroke? How awful! He was so young. The funeral will be packed. Did you ask the priest when the service will be?" Sometimes my parents would turn to me. "Do you remember Mrs. Petit? She was Jean's wife, you know, the man who played the trumpet in the brass band. She died last night. She was so fond of you."

◇◇◇◇

"DID ANYONE DIE TODAY?" Although my brother and I heard this question every day, the discussions between my parents in the living room or around the dinner table were mostly uplifting. Conversations jumped from upcoming funerals to the latest quote for a remains transfer, flower arrangements for the afternoon burial, coffin plates to give to the funeral parlor, how deep a vault had to be dug, short messages that clients wanted affixed to the memorial plaque, headstone lettering that had to be redone by All Saints' Day, a monument delivery from the south of France scheduled for the following day, and so on.

Some might assume I was traumatized by the funereal atmosphere that provided the backdrop for my childhood. But in all honesty, it seemed completely normal for my parents to discuss death at the dinner table. All parents talk about their professional lives in front of their children; it would be impossible not to. We all bring work home, except perhaps if we're secret service agents. My parents were no different, and who can blame them? I might have found their world odd if our home hadn't shared a wall with the monument shop; I wouldn't have understood the sober nature of their work. Looking back, I'm sure it was growing up in this environment and watching my parents do their jobs that helped me feel comfortable around death while I played *Tetris* on my Game Boy.

In high school, I spent summer vacations working with my father in cemeteries around Bray-sur-Seine. These were lifeless, charmless, grassless cemeteries, most often located in the middle of nowhere, far from the nearest town. Very few trees grew along the gravel-covered paths, and a monument to the dead occasionally stood at the center of the grounds. Empty laundry detergent containers serving as watering cans were often piled in a heap by the only spigot, right where you walked in. If you were lucky, you might find squat toilets on site; otherwise, you had to go in the neighboring field. This was the backdrop against which I helped my father and his day laborers dig graves, prepare vaults, or install funeral monuments.

I enjoyed the calm of these deserted cemeteries, far from the bustle of cities and towns. It was there that I learned the art of cement mixing as well as how to bend my knees when digging, rake with a straight back, and operate the truck-mounted crane when I was allowed.

We always ran into at least one familiar face who'd take the opportunity to say hello to my father—and find out who had died recently. Cemeteries were social places: we chatted about the dead and swapped the latest village gossip. It was in a cemetery that I learned how to shoot the breeze, speak solemnly of the dead, lead with a kind word, and—when my father permitted it—use humor to relieve tension.

⋄⋄⋄⋄

LIVING IN CLOSE PROXIMITY to death never seemed unusual. I can honestly say that I had a perfectly ordinary childhood. My parents always had a lot of friends, and nobody ever reported them to social services. Their business didn't hamper my social life. My friends never made fun of me because my parents were undertakers. Nor did I ever feel the need to play up my circumstances by dressing goth or becoming a horror movie buff. In the end, being the son of the village headstone maker was no different than being the son of the village butcher. Nobody cared, least of all me.

Despite growing up in this unusual environment, I never wanted to work in the funeral industry or take over the family business. And my parents didn't push me to. I was a good student, so they encouraged me to continue my studies. I decided to pursue a university degree without really knowing what I wanted to do. I chose law because it was such a broad field.

And because I'd heard the law opens many doors.

Fashion Victims

UNDER NAPOLEON'S 1804 decree, burial concessions were rare privileges reserved for France's elite. Yet over time, they would replace the individual plots each municipality was required to offer its citizens, free of charge, for a five-year period. Beginning January 1, 1874, the Paris government ruled that temporary concessions would only be offered in cemeteries that lay outside city limits; as a result, perpetual concessions became the only type of burial permitted at Père-Lachaise. The new regulation marked a turning point for the cemetery, whose plots were suddenly reserved for wealthy Parisians who could afford them. This remained the case until 2003, when the cemetery began to offer shorter concessions.

The rise in paid concessions kicked off a surge in commemorative art. While the 1804 decree permitted individuals to erect memorial monuments, the first tombs were modest, often a simple headstone in a grassy enclosure. It wasn't until the second half of the nineteenth century that funerary art reached its golden age. Prominent families abandoned any semblance of sobriety, building grandiose monuments to show off their social status and celebrate their success. "To be buried in Père-Lachaise is like having mahogany furniture. It is a sign of elegance," wrote Victor Hugo in *Les Misérables*.

The tombs most emblematic of this period are funeral chapels, or monuments built to resemble miniature houses of worship. These popular memorials sit on top of vaults large enough to accommodate extended families. They feature an altar and a prie-dieu, so visitors can come pay their respects. The first, designed by Brongniart himself for the Greffulhe family (known for inspiring the works of Marcel Proust), paved the way for many chapels to follow, reshaping the landscape and considerably reducing the cemetery's greenery. While Paris was being transformed by the Haussmann style of architecture during Napoleon III's Second Empire, Père-Lachaise was experiencing a similar metamorphosis as neat rows of funeral chapels began lining its avenues.

<><><><>

ALTHOUGH CEMETERIES CONTINUE to serve a hygienic purpose, many have come to regard them primarily as commemorative spaces. As people slowly turn away from religion—and with it, the prospect of a life after death—

cemeteries are increasingly called on to help the bereaved cope with the loss of a loved one. Our job is to make sure these people are remembered through gravestones and other material expressions. We do everything in our power to evoke their memory and stay connected to them. Proving our love through simple acts like cleaning their tombs and planting flowers helps to keep the dead present in our lives. It also reminds us that we'll eventually join our loved ones in death.

Perhaps living on in memory is the only real life after death. In her book *Living With Our Dead*, Rabbi Delphine Horvilleur notes that the Hebrew word for "cemetery" means "house of the living." I believe it's a fitting description: the tombstones and epitaphs of our loved ones afford them a second life by evoking their memory. They won't fall into oblivion as long as someone is alive to remember them. Writer Jean d'Ormesson expressed this sentiment perfectly: "There is something stronger than death—it is the presence of the absent in the memory of the living and the transmission, to those yet unborn, of the name, the glory, the power, and the joy of those who have left us, who live forever in the minds and in the hearts of those who remember."

◇◇◇◇◇

AND YET, LIKE tombstones that crumble over time, maybe the struggle to be remembered, though commendable, is an illusory one. Renowned figures of the political, military, industrial, scientific, and artistic elite attempted to thwart this inescapable fate. To keep their legacy alive for centuries to come, they erected elaborate mausoleums often featuring a bust or statue in their likeness to pay tribute to their genius. Funerary art proliferated, as if art alone could triumph over death and preserve their memory for all eternity. This obsession with posterity yielded many allegorical masterpieces of the day. You can find Chapu's *La Pensée* and his *Le Génie de l'Immortalité* on the graves of Marie d'Agoult (known under the pen name Daniel Stern) and philosopher Jean Reynaud, respectively. Plaster casts of Préault's *Le Silence*, commissioned for the tomb of Jacob Roblès, are on display at the Louvre and the Musée Carnavalet. Saint-Marceaux's *Le Devoir* figures on the monument to politician Pierre Tirard, and Mercié's *L'Histoire* is sculpted into historian Jules Michelet's mausoleum. Barrias's *La Douleur* sits atop architect Antoine Guérinot's resting place, and the list could go on.

Père-Lachaise features tombs of all styles, from simple rounded headstones to Gothic chapels and sarcophagi inspired by ancient Egypt. Like the works mentioned above, a number of funeral monuments were designed by celebrated architects (Eugène Viollet-le-Duc, Louis Visconti) and sculptors (David d'Angers, Albert Bartholomé, René de Saint-Marceaux, Jules Dalou, Antoine Étex), making Père-Lachaise not only a burial ground for luminaries but also an open-air museum.

Statues, effigies, busts, and other grave markers suffuse the cemetery with humanity. It's impossible to avoid the human forms that people the grounds, many of which have become familiar landmarks that guide me through the labyrinthine space. Their presence is reassuring; while

the vegetation changes with the seasons, nature seems to have no hold over these bodies frozen in time. Their joyless faces catch your eye, and each time I look at them a sort of melancholy overtakes me. The busts often appear stern, while the statues look forlorn, their eyes lowered. The anguished expressions of the caryatids and other mourners reflect the immense pain of losing a loved one. The tomb of François-Vincent Raspail, for example, depicts his grief-stricken wife bidding the chemist goodbye, covered in a shroud and clinging to the bars of the prison where he is held captive. The gravity of these works gives Père-Lachaise a sacred aura and prompts visitors to exercise the same restraint they would in a museum or cathedral.

AS FUNERAL MONUMENT PRODUCTION industrialized over the twentieth century, the tradition of creating grandiose works of art waned. Today, even the wealthiest families rarely commission ostentatious memorials. Vanity has been shelved; restraint is now the fashion. We could interpret this postmortem humility as a welcome sign of democratization that has leveled the playing field between the dead: no matter who we were or what we did, we'll all end up in more or less similar graves.

But as the curator of a cemetery known for its exceptional architecture, I consider this funerary timidity to be rather regrettable. Père-Lachaise wouldn't be such a remarkable place if megalomania hadn't once driven the most fortunate to have tombs erected in the image of their bloated pride. Standardization is affecting more than just Père-Lachaise; cemeteries across France are having tombs mass-produced and shipped to them from factories in China or India. As a result, they're beginning to look like planned subdivisions—homogenous, soulless tracts of land where cookie-cutter homes stretch out in long, drab rows. Nobody

An open-air museum

Père-Lachaise is a veritable showcase for funerary art. It benefits from two levels of protection.

- *Classified heritage.* There are fourteen classified historical monuments, which receive the highest level of protection: the Communards' Wall, the semicircular entrance gate, the East Chapel, Albert Bartholomé's *Monument to the Dead*, and nine tombs, including those of Molière, La Fontaine, Chopin, Oscar Wilde, and Abelard and Heloise.

- *Registered heritage.* The building that houses the crematorium and columbarium, designed by architect Jean-Camille Formigé, has been registered as a historical monument since 1995. All monuments built before 1900 located in Divisions 1–58, 65–71, and 91 are also registered, totaling some thirty thousand tombs. The families who own these plots aren't permitted to alter them without prior approval from the regional Conservation of Historical Monuments office.

visits these bedroom communities; they are of little interest to nonresidents. Cemeteries are gradually losing their charm in the same way, serving no purpose other than to house the graves of those buried there. The tombs themselves lack symbolism, with merely a name engraved to mark a life lived. Increasingly, cemeteries are becoming sad places that nobody—living or dead—wants to visit. It's understandable that some would prefer their ashes to be scattered at sea, perhaps near a favorite vacation spot, instead of having their bodies laid to rest in a characterless plot of earth.

Unfortunately, municipalities are powerless to fight the increasing uniformity of commemorative art. Cemeteries can't compel people to choose aesthetically interesting monuments, any more than they can control their shapes or materials. Some cemeteries try to break the monotony of perfectly aligned, identical tombstones by playing with the common areas—grassing over paths, adding flower beds, or planting trees. Sometimes, these laudable intentions result in beautifully landscaped cemeteries whose lush greenery makes them havens of peace and whose opulent foliage sets the tone for a quiet stroll to honor the departed.

◇◇◇◇◇

TO PRESERVE THE QUALITY of its landscape from any major alterations, Père-Lachaise has been granted specific legal protections. The oldest and most picturesque section of the cemetery has been designated a classified site since 1962. The section that includes its more recent divisions was named a registered site in 1975. These safeguards ensure that Père-Lachaise will retain its unique character. In short, that it will stay Père-Lachaise.

Any new monument must be approved by a Buildings of France architect prior to construction. This governing body is tasked with preserving France's heritage landscapes and historical monuments and has the authority to reject or amend certain projects. That said, most families who purchase a plot today tend to opt for a simple design—a reflection, they often say, of their loved one. Commissioned works of commemorative art have become quite rare.

Père-Lachaise has nevertheless carried out a handful of unusual projects in recent years that have raised some eyebrows. For example, photographer André Chabot restored an abandoned chapel and placed a giant black granite camera inside. A QR code on the outer wall links to his website, La Mémoire nécropolitaine (Necropolitan Memory), which boasts an impressive catalog of photos of… grave sites. Stroll further up into the hills of Père-Lachaise and you'll come across the striking mausoleum of now-retired pharmacist Jean-Louis Sacchet. Fascinated by all things Egyptian, Sacchet built himself a pyramid and decorated the inside walls with frescoes and hieroglyphics. It's no surprise he told the newspaper *Libération* that he's planning to be mummified following a very strict procedure. More recently, in 2021 novelist Violaine Vanoyeke commissioned a life-size statue of herself made of white Carrara marble. It had the desired effect—now everyone refers to her as the "white lady."

These three tombs, whose owners are still very much alive, stand out for their exceptionality. In the presence of such works of art, it's hard not to wonder what our own resting places would look like if we were to design them. It's a question few people ask themselves. To think of your grave is to think of your death. It forces you to project yourself into the next life and consider how you want to be remembered by those you leave behind.

An Unusual Job

AT EIGHTEEN, I moved out of my parents' home and into a university residence in Melun, about an hour away. I left the funeral monument business to discover the world of law, which would keep me busy for the next five years—five marvelous years spent studying the body of legislation that governs our lives and society. In 2004, I graduated with a master's degree in literary, artistic, and industrial property law from Paris-Panthéon-Assas University.

Over the next two years, I worked as an in-house lawyer in the audiovisual industry, stringing together a series of underpaid internships and temporary contracts. It was a thankless job where I had to play the role of the villain, curbing directors' enthusiasm, obtaining the necessary filming permits, reminding filmmakers of the risk of copyright infringement, and so on. In-house lawyers are indispensable pains-in-the-ass.

The work wasn't uninteresting, but I soon realized the harsh reality of the professional world wasn't nearly as stimulating as the academic world I'd left behind. I started questioning my career path. I wasn't really enjoying myself and felt lost. I decided I wanted to try something new—I was still young, after all, and I had my whole life ahead of me. I signed up to take a civil service exam for the City of Paris, which I passed. I'd been drawn to administrative law during my studies, and I realized that the values underpinning public service seemed to better match my own.

Since I'd received one of the highest scores on the exam, I theoretically had my pick of vacant positions. But from the very beginning, the recruiter I'd been assigned took great pains to suggest a position he felt I'd be good at given my background in law. It was clear from the way he tiptoed around it and carefully weighed each word that he was required to fill the position with someone from my cohort. "It's an unusual job. It doesn't attract many candidates, but the work is really very interesting. I think you should apply—with your law degree, you'd be a great fit..."

I was intrigued; what was so peculiar about the job that seemed to put off so many candidates? I asked the recruiter the question he'd been expecting. "So, what exactly is the position?" He continued his description, looking a bit uncomfortable and avoiding eye contact, before finally admitting that the job title was assistant general counsel for the City of Paris Division of Cemeteries. "Your office would be located in Père-Lachaise."

At that moment, I knew I'd made the right decision to change careers. My eyes sparkled. My face broke into a smile. Without skipping a beat, I told him I was very interested. I didn't even wait to hear further details. The recruiter looked back at me in surprise. He confessed that I was the first to apply for this "very attractive position" and hurried to extol its long list of virtues, as if he feared I might change my mind. I told him it sounded great, that my parents worked in the funeral industry, and that I was very eager to apply. Since all candidates were required to apply for three empty positions, I had to take job descriptions from two other sectors. But this was only a formality; before I'd even interviewed for the "unusual" position whose work was "really very interesting," I knew it was the job for me.

◇◇◇◇

I CALLED MY PARENTS as soon as I left the recruiter's office. "Guess where I'll be working if I get the first job they put me up for? I'm so happy I could die!" Unfortunately, my parents didn't get the hint. Like everyone else, they had no idea municipal offices could be located in a place like Père-Lachaise, and they never imagined that their son would be working in the funeral industry in Paris. When I told them the good news, they couldn't believe their ears. They were just as surprised as I was and delighted in my incredible stroke of luck.

I was the only person to apply for the "unusual job." Nobody else wanted to work for the Division of Cemeteries, where they were convinced their résumés would collect dust. "You're digging your own grave, man!" a classmate warned, thinking he was being funny. "It's one of the worst departments in the city!" With his comment ringing in my ears, it dawned on me that my colleagues didn't consider the funeral industry an attractive sector. I'd somehow made it through childhood without ever feeling the sting, but suddenly I was listening to someone scoff at my desire to work in death care. The vast majority of my peers were hoping for a position in more prestigious departments, like Finance or HR. Moreover, rumor had it that the bonuses weren't very appealing. But I hadn't chosen to work for the City to advance my career or make a fortune; I'd done it to give meaning to my life. And paradoxically, a cemetery was the perfect place for that.

◇◇◇◇◇

WHEN I INTERVIEWED with the department head and his assistant, we understood each other immediately. The fact that my parents were memorial stonemasons came up right away. There was no need to explain the difference between a plot, vault, and crypt, or explain the importance of All Saints' Day. I already knew how to give grieving families the respect they deserved. Above all, I was struck by the obvious passion these professionals had for their department. To them, this wasn't just a job; it was their life's work. Their enthusiasm was contagious, and I told them on my way out that I was eager to begin as soon as possible. Throughout my career, I've often sensed a similar passion among funeral professionals. Few other sectors can boast the same.

IN MAY 2006, I stepped through the gates of Père-Lachaise and entered the remarkable world of Parisian cemeteries. For four years, I served as counsel in what is essentially the legal department for all twenty of the city's cemeteries. The office is tasked with standardizing funeral regulations and managing the city's 634,000 concession agreements. When I arrived, the director had just been transferred to another department. It took months to fill his position, for the same reasons that filling my own had proved such a challenge. I had to learn to manage the department on my own, with help from the four administrative staff who worked there.

Just like my experience in the private sector, my new role had its downsides. That's the nature of law: it's impossible to please everyone. The worst part was having to refuse a burial when the deceased held no legal right to the tomb in which their loved ones wanted them interred. Explaining this to a grieving family requires a fair amount of tact; the news can be a tough pill to swallow. Choosing the right words and tone of voice is just as important as being a good listener. It didn't always go well, despite my best efforts to ease the delivery. Death is very personal, and I sometimes touched a nerve. A few families threatened to beat the hell out of me or dump the coffin on my desk. Others told me I had no heart to say such a thing to a widow. Unhappy mourners often reminded me that their tax dollars paid my salary; some even told me to watch my back because they "knew people." I owe my worst memory to the family of a celebrated writer who, after listening to my position, assured me they understood the legal grounds that prohibited me from authorizing their loved one's burial. They even thanked me for the straightforward explanation I'd given them over the phone. Our interaction ended on a very cordial note. The following week, they sent a scathing letter to the head of the cemeteries department—with a copy to the mayor of Paris!

◇◇◇◇◇

I REMAINED UNDETERRED. The law is harsh, but it's the law. Even for the dead. As the legal counsel assigned to cemeteries, my job was to enforce cemetery department procedures without qualms or hesitation. Luckily, it was relatively rare for tensions to run high. The vast majority of the time, I helped families resolve legal issues regarding their burial plots. Since death is a taboo subject, many families are reluctant to discuss it and find themselves at a loss when a loved one dies. Often, my team and I acted as problem-solvers. My decisions and advice had a direct impact on families, and I knew from their heartfelt thanks that I provided concrete, invaluable support. Concessions contracts were much more interesting than the ones I'd drafted for the reality TV contestants at my last job. For the first time in my short career, I'd stopped wondering why I got up each morning. My work was meaningful.

Another advantage of my first job at Père-Lachaise was that it plunged me back into the wonderful world of the death care industry that I'd left eight years prior. Every morning, I went to work in a cemetery. My days were spent discussing the deceased and their needs: coffins, vaults, burial rights, cremation, urns, remains transfers, grave recycling, and more. Topics I'd heard my own parents and grandparents discuss countless times. I hadn't chosen to take over the family business, but somehow I'd still wound up in the same field. A part of me now believes in fate. Death grabbed me by the collar—not to finish me off, but to keep me close. Had it missed me? Did it need me? Perhaps. The fact that I'm still here is proof it has no regrets.

Let's hope our story lasts awhile longer.

A Stroll Among the Graves

Unlike the cemeteries of the Ancien Régime whose gates were kept under lock and key, Père-Lachaise was designed from the outset to be open to the public. Its natural beauty quickly attracted more than just grieving families. From its earliest days, Parisians who didn't even own a plot came to stroll and find refuge in its sprawling grounds. The city had yet to establish a system of public parks, and Père-Lachaise was the only large green space available to residents until the Parc des Buttes-Chaumont opened in 1867.

Tellingly, the term "cemetery" would be dropped from its name over time. Local residents, particularly from the neighboring municipalities of Belleville, Charonne, and Ménilmontant, took to calling the former site of the Jesuit retreat after its most famous and beloved occupant. They naturally moved away from the official "Cemetery of the East" in favor of "Père-Lachaise Cemetery" before settling on simply "Père-Lachaise." To Parisians, this familiarity underscored the fact that the site was more than just a necropolis, and that its popular function largely outstripped its original purpose.

Although most of Père-Lachaise's visitors today consist of tourists and celebrity grave hunters, the cemetery attracts a wide range of people. Thanks to the countless hours I've spent observing and chatting to visitors, I've developed a rough categorization, which is, of course, subjective and

Pop quiz

Who am I?
Hint: A famous Jesuit

Born in 1624 at the Château d'Aix, I was the great-nephew of Father Coton, confessor of Henry IV of France. After joining the Society of Jesus as a teen, I went to Lyon to study at Collège de la Trinité, where I later taught philosophy.

In 1675, I moved back to Paris and became the confessor of Louis XIV, a position I held for more than thirty years. Although I lived on Rue Saint-Antoine, I would spend long stretches at the Jesuits' country retreat at Mont-Louis. I developed a fondness for the property, which I gradually expanded and landscaped over time, thanks to the Sun King's generosity.

caricatural by nature. Some of you might recognize yourselves in more than one category. Let's go for a stroll among the graves.

◇◇◇◇◇

THE FIRST TYPE we come across are the locals, who flood Père-Lachaise as though it's the neighborhood park; they can be found reading on a bench or taking a Sunday afternoon family walk. With its five gates, the cemetery is also a handy shortcut to access the 11th and 20th arrondissements during opening hours.

Nearly one hundred years after my death, the estate was purchased by the City of Paris and transformed into a vast necropolis that has become a world-famous resting place for countless celebrities. Eventually, Parisians stopped using its official title, the Cemetery of the East, and started referring to it simply by my name. I am…

François d'Aix de La Chaize, more commonly known as Père Lachaise. I am not buried in the place that bears my name; I died in 1709 at Mont-Louis, long before it was converted into a cemetery in 1804. I was laid to rest alongside my Jesuit brothers in the Church of Saint-Paul-Saint-Louis, but over time my name has become synonymous with the famous burial grounds.

Then there are the regulars who come by every day and proudly call themselves "Pèrelachaisians." They are often retired and spend a great deal of their free time wandering the cobblestone paths, meeting in small groups to discuss the latest gossip or to trade rumors heard whispered along the lanes. Pèrelachaisians also enjoy helping lost tourists and will gladly point the way to the graves of Honoré de Balzac or Édith Piaf. Whenever the press releases the burial information of a celebrity, they come early to get a front-row seat. Once there, they'll gather to reminisce about the funerals they've attended. "I went to Bécaud and Bashung, but I missed Delpech..." Knowing Père-Lachaise inside and out makes them excellent sources; I've gotten more than one hot tip from this crowd.

Pèrelachaisians shouldn't be confused with another category of regulars: the flaneurs. They come less often, sometimes from quite far afield, to enjoy an afternoon alone in the cemetery's bucolic setting. Père-Lachaise is their refuge from the outside world. Away from the hustle and bustle of life in Paris, flaneurs are content to meander aimlessly through the cemetery's maze of walkways with only their thoughts to guide them. But there's nothing woebegone about their ambling. Père-Lachaise offers a poetic backdrop whose tranquility nourishes their soul; the tombs give free rein to their existential reveries. Why do we live? Why do we die? What is the meaning of life?

The more discreet "taphophiles" are another type of visitor we see regularly. These tourists have a fascination with—you guessed it—epitaphs. Such an unusual passion might make them seem eccentric to the average person. But we have to thank these enthusiasts for shedding light on certain tombs and the stories associated with them. With its 96,600 graves, Père-Lachaise is the ideal playground for taphophiles around the world. Their greatest victory is identifying the resting place of some long-forgotten historical figure beneath a grave marker overgrown with weeds, its words lost to the elements.

Another group of visitors comes to wander the grounds and listen for the mewing of the cemetery's stray cats. Père-Lachaise's feline population has been around for decades, even though Montmartre is the cemetery in Paris most famous for its cats. You might pity these strays, forced to hunt birds for survival unlike their house cat cousins who are fed three square meals a day. Think again! The cats at Père-Lachaise are in excellent health, thanks to the cemetery's many "cat ladies." Who are these Good Samaritans, and how are they organized? It's difficult to say; they have a wide range of profiles and motivations. And, like midwives, on rare occasions the cat *ladies* turn out to be men. Their only commonality is their immeasurable love for the strays of Père-Lachaise (and the fact that most already have several cats at home). Their furry friends, often nicknamed things like Fluffy, Bandit, and Ranger, know their feeding times and locations by heart. The greediest nose their way into more than one bowl. These kind souls deserve our collective thanks for offering the cemetery cats such a good life.

More surprising still, Père-Lachaise attracts a great many lovers. With its enchanting backdrop and its residents' discretion guaranteed, there's no better place in Paris for a romantic tryst. Untold love stories have blossomed in its leafy shadows, and a number of people owe their existence to Père-Lachaise's magnetism. What could be more swoon-worthy than a first kiss in front of the tomb of Abelard and Heloise? In an article published in *Le Temps* in 1896, journalist Adolphe Brisson mentioned seeing lovers in the cemetery during an interview with the curator at the time:

> As we speak, [he] observes visitors making their way toward deserted walkways. He points out a very elegant young woman whose clipped pace suggests obvious concern. She turns, retraces her steps... She is looking for someone or is late for a rendezvous. "I assume," he turns to me, "the lass isn't here for a chat with the dead!" Soon enough the long-awaited party appears and approaches... She smiles. He looks upon her with longing. The two shadows walk off slowly, side by side. Love, like roses, blooms among the tombs.

In addition to lovers embracing, you might come across photographers hoping for the perfect shot or small groups of art students seated on benches or on the ground. Heads bent diligently over their sketch pads, they practice placing the vanishing point along the horizon line. This is the cemetery at its most studious.

Unfortunately, Père-Lachaise welcomes more than just the quiet, unobtrusive figures you might glimpse among its silent and shaded paths. Certain visitors living with mental health issues are attracted to the cemetery's mysticism, as if it holds the key to their fixations. I've occasionally had to call for help with a mental health crisis. Once, a gentleman staging a sit-in at the administrative offices hurled insults at me. "You gonna bury me alive and saw off my head? Are you the Antichrist? I wanna be buried in Père-Lachaise! Dial 0145—that's God's number!" Another man, fists bloodied after trying to punch through the ceramic tiles of a chapel, insisted it was really a portal to another world where all his problems would be solved. Once, a woman shouted that she had proof I was in cahoots with the CIA after I refused to give her information about a grave she claimed was her mother's. On a more somber note, one morning a pair of tourists notified us that a man had hanged himself from a tree in front of Oscar Wilde's grave.

While these people are clearly struggling with their mental health, the same can't be said for the slew of pseudo artists who think they're being subversive by posing in provocative clothing—or completely naked, in some cases—along walkways or inside the chapels themselves. Not everyone's got talent. The dead deserve our respect.

Even more worrisome are the exhibitionists who take advantage of the cemetery's maze of walkways and its myriad hiding spots. It's always distressing to hear from the victims of their criminal behavior. City police have made several arrests since 2020, with subsequent convictions. I also receive complaints from families who are shocked to come across a sexual encounter in the Maréchaux sector, known in the gay community for being a favorite hookup spot.

MY TEAM AND I work hard to ensure that these different groups coexist harmoniously, without disturbing the bereaved who come to Père-Lachaise for a burial, a cremation service, or to visit the grave of a loved one. Death opens deep wounds in the living, making emotions run high: grief, anger, denial, stress, depression—the list goes on. Supporting mourners through this painful period requires good listening skills and a great deal of empathy. They are Père-Lachaise's top priority despite being in the minority, and every effort is made to ensure the cemetery is well maintained and offers a quiet sanctuary to support the grieving process.

On the whole, these groups share the space in relative peace. The vast majority of visitors have an almost automatic reflex to dress and behave appropriately. Thankfully, displays of impropriety are few and far between when compared to the high volume of traffic, though cemetery staff bring various incidents to my attention daily. Unfortunately, most of the complaints involve theft of some kind: flowers, plaques, inscriptions, trinkets, and even the batteries from LED grave candles. Others involve disturbing behavior. One guest wrote that as he was heading to the columbarium to pay his respects, he heard a tourist shout, "It smells like something's burning!" A remark the rest of his group found hilarious. Others complain—rightly so—about people picnicking between the graves, playing *Pokémon Go* tournaments along the paths, or sunbathing on the lawn reserved for scattering ashes.

Clashes between users came to a head during the second and third pandemic lockdowns, which took place in

November 2020 and April 2021 respectively. While COVID-19 turned a spotlight on cemeteries due to the dramatic number of deaths, it also prompted people living in big cities to take an interest in exploring these curious places.

During the lockdowns, Parisians were barred from going to cinemas, theaters, pools, gyms, or museums. They were also forced to stay within a certain radius of their home. Since the weather was sunny and mild, many residents took the opportunity to rediscover Père-Lachaise. Some days saw more than ten thousand visitors walk through the cemetery gates. The same period marked an uptick in inappropriate behavior: picnics on the grass (or even on the tombstones), tanning sessions on the lawn of the Casimir-Perier roundabout, people jogging, children playing hide-and-seek inside the funeral chapels, photo shoots, alcohol and drug abuse, and more. It made life difficult for the security guards. Parents who lost their children would wander about shouting, "Marcelline! Fernand! Where are you?" One little Mathias had to be picked up and comforted by a security guard while his colleagues went off in search of the parents. A woman who owned a plot wrote to complain that Père-Lachaise was starting to feel more and more like the temporary artificial beaches of Paris-Plages.

Once the lockdowns were lifted, there was a significant drop in these conflicts of interest. Nonetheless, to remind visitors they were entering a place of mourning, we posted signage that included pictograms at the different entrances to explain the cemetery rules. My colleague designed this sheet. Though often ridiculed, it has since achieved a sort of cult status, and it sends a straightforward message: inappropriate behavior will not be tolerated. When security guards have to contend with the occasional aggressive visitor, whining and carping about their right to jog or cycle through the cemetery, they can simply point to a pictogram rather than rattle off the seventy articles of Paris cemetery regulations. Now more than ever, making sure different types of visitors can peacefully coexist within the cemetery walls poses a daily challenge.

Bubbles of Hope

A FEW MONTHS EARLIER...
It was March 17, 2020, and the government of France had just instituted its first lockdown. Hospitals were teeming with patients, and the number of deaths linked to the new virus was rising daily. My colleagues and I felt powerless as we watched footage from Italy, where cemeteries were overflowing and funeral parlors were overwhelmed. The wave was coming, and we knew it would be terrible. When a major crisis hits the nation, death follows. Heat waves, terrorist attacks—the millennium so far is rife with examples.

In these critical moments, the various players in the death care chain spring into action. On March 17, despite the worry written all over their faces, every Père-Lachaise employee showed up to work. The previous day, the municipal government had decided to close all Paris cemeteries until further notice. Only funeral processions were allowed through the gates, and even these were limited to a twenty-person maximum. For eight consecutive weeks, Père-Lachaise ceased to be a refuge for grieving families and a garden oasis for Parisians in search of green space, much less a magnet for tourists from around the world. Its role was reduced to its primary and, for the time being, only function: burying the dead.

The dreaded wave arrived at the beginning of April, about two weeks after lockdown began. The number of daily burials soared. By the end of the month, they would rise by 40 percent in Père-Lachaise alone. The crematorium's furnaces were operating seven days a week. The office's phone was ringing off the hook, and its inbox was flooded with emails. Funeral parlors wanted information in order to plan services. Families wanted to know whether their plots had enough space for another coffin or urn. Some told us they were expecting a loved one to die at any moment.

The tension was palpable among the team, whose numbers had plummeted for various reasons: confirmed cases, contact cases, isolation for the immunocompromised. Reinforcements from other Paris cemeteries came to help out at Père-Lachaise; they stayed for several weeks to support the only two administrative staff on hand. Without their efforts, burials would have been backlogged for some time. Paris's motto, *Fluctuat nec mergitur* ("She is tossed by the waves, but does not sink"), had never seemed so fitting.

Meanwhile, we scrambled to get our hands on masks, hand sanitizer, and disinfectant spray as quickly as possible. But the biggest struggle was having to reconsider our relationships with others and rethink the way we socialized. Keep your distance. Don't shake hands. Stay six feet apart. Follow the safety and prevention measures. Wear a mask and make sure it covers your nose. View the world through a plexiglass screen or fogged-up glasses. Keep your fear in check. Don't let your anxiety show. Get used to not seeing smiles. Gloves or no gloves? Unlearn social cues. Stagger your lunch breaks. Attend a string of crisis management meetings. Stay in your bubble. See your colleagues only on screen from the waist up. Remember to mute yourself during a video call. Familiarize yourself with expressions like incubation period, chain of transmission, contact tracing, community spread, social distancing, and more.

◇◇◇◇◇

IT WAS UNDER these surreal circumstances that on the afternoon of April 23, I went out to check on a plot I was about to issue to a new family. I wound my way through the romantic sector of a deserted Père-Lachaise. It struck me, as it always does, how poetry can emerge from such a chaotic place. I listened to the birdsong, mostly blackbirds marking their territory. Somewhere a green woodpecker sounded the alarm; no doubt it had spotted me. Suddenly, my attention was drawn to a rustling sound coming from a patch of undergrowth to my right. I was intrigued. I could see the tall grasses moving, but I couldn't determine what was causing the disturbance. At first, I thought it was a cat. Although they tend to be shy, I frequently come across the cemetery cats on my walks. But when a head popped up from the brush, it wasn't a cat I found staring back at me.

With its pointed nose and ears and greyish-red fur, the animal looked a bit like a dog. But—no! It was a fox cub! I wasn't dreaming. A baby fox was watching me, just feet away from where I was rooted to the spot. We stared at each other, neither one moving, our eyes wide in surprise. I was the first human it had ever seen, and it was the first fox I'd come across in Père-Lachaise. My heart started to race, and my chest tightened. I was overcome with joy at the sight of this wild animal. Very carefully, I took my phone out of my pants pocket and snapped a couple of pictures before it scampered off to its den.

This unexpected encounter touched me on several levels. I was flooded with excitement, but I also felt extremely lucky. I could have taken a thousand other routes to get to my destination, but I happened to be passing through this seldom-visited area of the cemetery at the same time the cub ventured out of its den—in broad daylight—to discover the world around it.

I returned to the spot around nine o'clock that same evening, anxious to find my new friend. Only this time, I brought my camera. It was still there, and just as I'd suspected, it wasn't alone. Four adorable fox pups were frolicking among the graves, right before my eyes. Crouching behind a tree so as not to frighten them, I made myself as discreet as possible and watched the spectacle unfold. Contorting my body to avoid detection, I managed to snap a few pictures. The boldest of the group came toward me, stopping mere feet from my hiding spot. I knelt there, frozen like the statues around me, and the fox didn't see me.

I'll always think back to that evening with fondness. It was the first piece of good news I'd been able to share since the lockdown began. The following weekend, two of my photographs were posted on Twitter and went viral. Several media features followed, including a television news segment on the program *Envoyé spécial* in late May. The foxes of Père-Lachaise had become stars. To my great pride, one of the photos I'd taken that night then made the front page of the newspaper *Le Parisien*. Since lockdown had begun, news outlets had been posting images of wild animals roaming the deserted streets of cities and towns. Deer in Boissy-Saint-Léger, wild boar in Ajaccio, fin whales off the coast of Marseille, a puma in Santiago. Parisians were astounded to learn that the animals they rarely encountered beyond the pages of their children's books could live in a cemetery a stone's throw from their homes.

Suddenly, people were seeing Père-Lachaise in a new light. It was no longer just the closed-off necropolis where COVID-19 victims were being cremated and buried at an alarming rate. It was also the place where a family of foxes had decided to take up residence. In a desolate, petrified Paris that had withdrawn into itself, these balls of fur had become bubbles of hope.

The Tissue Box

MANY PEOPLE DREAM of securing a spot in Père-Lachaise while they're still alive. Plenty think it's impossible, that the cemetery is reserved for VIP guests. They're wrong, although it's no secret that plots are hard to come by. Because it's located within the Paris city limits, in the midst of a dense urban area, expanding Père-Lachaise is out of the question. It was enlarged five times between 1824 and 1850, back when the cemetery still sat outside the capital's borders. Every last inch was developed to meet growing demand for burial plots, often at the expense of vegetation. Today, around seventy thousand tombs are squeezed into its 110 acres. As Paris's population grew and family concessions became the standard, space at Père-Lachaise—and at all of the cemeteries within the city—was at a premium. To solve the problem, five large cemeteries were opened on the outskirts of Paris in the second half of the nineteenth century. Together, these cemeteries total nearly 1.3 square miles.

If a recently deceased Parisian who expressed an objection to cremation didn't already possess a family plot, it can be difficult to have them buried in Père-Lachaise. Acquiring a new plot is the only way to honor their wish to be buried, but space is limited. That said, the cemetery does repossess a handful of abandoned concessions each year and make them available to the public.

So, how do you go about securing one of these rare patches of earth? The moment one becomes available, the first family who calls the office will be given an appointment—provided the deceased resided in Paris. There are no other selection criteria; I don't ask for a cover letter or résumé, let alone a character reference. There is no waitlist. Chance, with its merciless objectivity, chooses for me. This protocol protects me from accusations of favoritism or corruption. Scarcity must be managed with care.

◇◇◇◇◇

IN MY FORMER CEMETERY, most transactions were conducted via funeral parlors. My staff met with the rare family who had an appointment. At Père-Lachaise, it's a different story. I am in charge of selling burial plots, for two main reasons.

The first is due to the site's uneven terrain and unique features: paved paths, many stairs, steep slopes, and dense undergrowth. Reaching a grave can prove complicated, especially once age begins to leave its mark. And although being buried near a shrub or tree can have its charms, there are downsides: moisture can cause moss to grow over the gravestone, which can also end up covered in rotting leaves or bird droppings. For these reasons, loved ones should see where a plot is located before the burial to avoid unpleasant surprises later on.

The second reason, mentioned earlier, is that the cemetery is a protected heritage site. Any new construction is subject to approval by a Buildings of France architect, meaning that families don't have total freedom to design a monument for their loved one. In fact, the project must meet very strict criteria. Polished granite, widely used today in many French cemeteries, is prohibited in Père-Lachaise. Bush-hammered granite, limestone, and white marble are the only authorized materials. It's important for families to be aware of these constraints, which vary according to the plot's location, so that they can make an informed purchase.

◇◇◇◇◇

WHEN I FIRST pictured myself meeting with grieving families, I imagined there would be lots of tears. It isn't hard to envision the sobbing and heartbreak associated with choosing a burial plot for a loved one and then seeing their final resting place for the first time. This is where the bereaved will go to pay their respects and leave flowers, trinkets, artwork, photos, or a poem, or where they might simply run an affectionate hand over the stone. For some, this meeting comes with the added weight of finding out where they themselves will be laid to rest alongside the loved one they're burying.

After I was appointed curator, one of the first items I purchased was a tissue box. But the tissue box in question couldn't simply be practical—it had to be decorative as well. For the first time in my life, I found myself scrolling through online catalogs full of tissue boxes, and I discovered a fascinating world. I had no idea there was such a wide variety of shapes, materials, and colors. There's a tissue box out there for everyone. After much research and a fair bit of hemming and hawing, I settled on a black faux-leather box that I believed would speak to the cemetery's reputation and character. Once it arrived, I placed it right in the center of the round table I use to conduct business with bereaved families.

◇◇◇◇◇

IN THE END, it was a bad investment. To my surprise, I discovered that people don't cry in my office. The families I meet with are seldom overwhelmed by grief. In fact, they're usually delighted to be there. They regularly sit across from me with big smiles on their faces and say things I never imagined I'd hear.

"We're very happy, thank you."

"That's wonderful! I'm so relieved to hear it."

"I can't thank you enough. This is the first piece of good news I've had in days."

"You can't imagine how thrilled we are. That's just fantastic."

"It was his dream, you know. He spent so much time in your cemetery. We're so grateful."

"Even in this awful time, I feel very fortunate thanks to you. God bless you, sir."

These are the words of families who had just lost a loved one. The one thing they all had in common? They were able to purchase a burial plot in Père-Lachaise.

Contrary to popular belief, it isn't only the rich or famous who find their way into my office. I meet with families

How much does a plot in Père-Lachaise cost?

The price of a standard burial space (approximately twenty square feet) is proportional to the length of the concession issued. Rates are set by the City of Paris; as of 2024, it costs €930 for ten years, €3,196 for thirty years, and €5,010 for fifty years. Perpetual concessions are priced at €16,829. This doesn't include the cost of building a vault and installing a monument, which can be quite expensive. Columbarium rates are more affordable, which is why many Parisians today are choosing to be cremated. A niche for three standard-sized urns costs €575 for ten years, €1,743 for thirty years, and €2,910 for fifty years. There is no fee to scatter ashes at Père-Lachaise; the popularity of the Memorial Garden lawn is owed more to economic reasons than to religious or philosophical ones.

from all social classes, faiths, and backgrounds. I can sell a ten-year concession to a family from a working-class neighborhood for under €1,000 on a Monday, and on Thursday sell a double plot to a multimillionaire for over €50,000 so he can build a family vault and grand mausoleum. Say what you want about death, one of its virtues is that it doesn't discriminate.

◇◇◇◇◇

AROUND A HUNDRED families walk into my office each year, which may seem like a lot. I'm often asked how I do it and if it gets depressing. But while these meetings are always emotional, a sense of joy predominates. As the above examples illustrate, the vast majority of people I meet with are happy in spite of the somber circumstances. Not only do they feel fortunate to have obtained a plot at Père-Lachaise, but they also have the satisfaction of being able to honor their loved one's last wishes in the best way possible. For many, Père-Lachaise is a prestigious cemetery, a five-star hotel for all eternity that will take good care of their loved ones. It's not uncommon for families to return a few days later with a box of chocolates as a token of their gratitude. A year to the day after I sold one widow a plot, she came by to tell me, "You saved my life!" Another to whom I'd just issued a concession brought me a pie she'd baked, along with an invitation to her husband's funeral. My presence, she said, would make her "very happy."

A FAMILY'S JOY at having secured a burial plot often sets the tone for our meeting. I'm always accompanied by Patrick, the cemetery's incomparable head gravedigger. He handles the logistics; I handle the paperwork. After finalizing the details in my office, we walk the family over to see their plot. Since concessions so seldom become available, there is never any choice. In other words, it's "take it or leave it"—though we'd never put it that way, of course! Once the families are standing in front of their plot, their reactions can be moving, tender, and, on occasion, surprising.

◇◇◇◇

"I CAN SEE our apartment from here! My husband will be right on the other side of the wall. It'll be like sleeping in separate rooms, really." For thirty years, this woman had lived with her husband in an apartment overlooking the cemetery. They'd promised each other they'd purchase a concession when one of them died. Amazingly, their wish had come true, and now each could continue watching over the other.

"It has a southern exposure? Easy enough to access, only three steps. The area seems nice and quiet; the graves are well maintained. I'm glad it's on the side by Place Gambetta; my sister never did like the 11th. There's a fair amount of privacy. And there's a nice view; you can even see the Eiffel Tower." Yes, sometimes we feel like real estate agents.

"It's a corner plot? That's perfect! My father loved corners." We didn't dare ask whether he'd been a boxer or if he simply loved curling up on his sectional sofa.

"I can't believe it! Look who's buried one plot over! The Singers!" This mother was crying tears of joy in the middle of the cemetery. In my office minutes before, she'd been telling us about her son who had died prematurely and how he'd loved music. She'd even shown us a video of him singing. We hadn't purposely chosen the plot next to the Singer family; some things are just meant to be.

"What a fabulous spot; it's just like him. He was amazing, you know. He was a very handsome man, truly brilliant, but so humble. He always did the right thing, wasn't one for the limelight. He was the best in his field, but he never liked to toot his own horn." After someone dies, it's common to remember only the positive and forget about their flaws. Sometimes, the list of superlatives is so long we begin to wonder whether the deceased was human like the rest of us.

"It's so calm and peaceful here, it almost makes you wish it was your turn." Almost.

◇◇◇◇

REACTIONS CAN BE comical, and it's not uncommon for the people we support through a very distressing time to break out in laughter or tell a joke or funny story about the

deceased. Patrick and I frequently have the impression that, oddly enough, these families are enjoying their time with us, that it serves as a kind of magical interlude during a tragic period. Many are also still in denial and haven't completely grasped the finality of death. This comes later, usually after the funeral.

I should point out, however, that not every meeting is lighthearted. For some people, a heavy cloud of heartbreak settles over the entire interaction. This is particularly common for families reeling from a violent death (an accident, suicide, or murder) or those burying a child. In other cases, tension within the family can make things difficult. When our time together turns into an opportunity to settle a score, I have to remind family members that it's neither the time nor the place. Once, a man was so incensed by a comment from his stepmother that he got up and left, slamming my office door on his way out. Fortunately, situations like this are rare.

Today, these meetings are my favorite part of the job. For a few moments, I'm able to devote all my time and energy to supporting these families as best I can. We exist in a bubble together, far from the day-to-day hassles and administrative headaches of running a cemetery. Though somber, these moments aren't unpleasant. Our genuine, sincere, and poignant discussions are what give meaning to my work.

Despite its futility, I can't bear to put my tissue box away—out of superstition, I suppose. So long as it's there, so long as it's not being used, my time spent with these families will retain that special, unique quality. And of course, sitting there between us, the tissue box sets the scene and the mood. It adds a human element and sends a signal to the families: this meeting is about more than paperwork—emotions are welcome too. The signatures and checkbook can wait. You're allowed to let go, express your grief, and sob, should you need. There are plenty of tissues.

You Can't Outfox a Fox

BABY FOXES IN the middle of Paris! Births in Père-Lachaise! This incredible expression of life among the graves prompted me to get back into photography, a hobby I'd mostly forgotten about since stepping into the role of curator. For the first two years on the job, I'd devoted nearly all of my time and energy to exploring every corner of the vast, labyrinthine space. Each day I learned more about its famous monuments, rich history, wealth of heritage, and other surprising aspects. I didn't have time for photography, especially since our family had just moved into the staff apartment and was busy with renovations. Last but not least, we'd also welcomed a new baby.

Nevertheless, my encounter with the fox made me want to dust off my camera and resurrect my Instagram account.

I jumped back online and followed the rules of social media, like any good disciple. Pretty soon, my account had attracted thousands of followers, and I can now say I'm an Instagram pro. To borrow from the epitaph on the tomb of Allan Kardec, founder of Spiritism—"To be born, to die, to be reborn again, and to constantly progress, such is the law"—my motto is:

TO LIKE, TO COMMENT, TO LIKE AGAIN,
AND TO CONSTANTLY POST, SUCH IS THE LAW.

As it turns out, taking pictures of fox cubs isn't an easy hobby. After all the media coverage, countless visitors came by wanting to know where their den was located. They thought they'd be able to snap a few pictures or even take some selfies, as if Père-Lachaise had become a zoo. Unfortunately for them, foxes are nocturnal and rarely come out during the day. Because I live on site, I'm able to observe and photograph them after the cemetery closes, when they're just beginning their day—or rather, their night. I take most of my pictures at dusk, between 8:45 and 9:15 PM.

The best time to see cubs is generally between mid-April and late May when, at around a month old, they'll venture beyond their den for the first time. Left to their own devices while their parents are off hunting, they frolic near home and await their return. In these moments, their curiosity is stronger than their mistrust. They walk over tombs or hide inside them, gnaw on low-hanging branches, sniff the air, stretch, yawn, lie down, prick up their ears at the slightest sound, and bound away in surprise. They develop their

senses and refine their motor skills, making the most of what the cemetery has to offer: a rocky expanse beneath a canopy of trees, conditions that resemble those found in the wild.

While it's heartwarming to watch foxes gambol about and explore the outside world during their early excursions, capturing these moments requires a great deal of patience. After the first two weeks, it can be harder and harder to catch them in action. Not only do the cubs become wary, but they also stray farther from the den as they learn to hunt for themselves. To continue observing them, I had to refine my skills. Naturally, the most basic precaution is to avoid making noise. To do this, I wear shoes with "quiet" soles and have developed an almost catlike way of moving. I avoid the cobblestones and keep to the edges of walkways, taking care to sidestep twigs and leaves that might compromise my position. My eyes scan the ground for obstacles; my feet adapt. My breathing slows as I approach my favorite sector. I can feel my heart beat in my chest. My body relaxes; my stress settles. I clear my head and control my emotions. I have to be ready once I get there. Only my hands are tensed around my camera, ready to spring into action the moment I glimpse the tip of a nose. When I arrive at the den, I hide behind a tree or crouch between two gravestones. I blend into the background and wait. Sometimes for quite a while. Sometimes for nothing. I always hope for the best. Tracking foxes requires the skills of a secret agent: artifice, patience, and discretion.

The wait can be painful. Very often, if I feel myself getting antsy, I tell myself, "Just five more minutes!" When one or more foxes suddenly appear, I only have a few seconds to snap some pictures before they disappear between the tombs. I'll always remember the emotion of those early scenes: the cubs playing, fighting, running, biting, or rolling on the ground before taking off like a shot. The fox pup that walked right under my nose and threw me a sidelong glance, proudly clenching a piece of marble cake in his mouth (where did that come from?). The father that suddenly burst into view clutching a pigeon in its jaws, followed by a horde of furious crows. The mother basking peacefully on a headstone, eyes unfocused, as if she were contemplating the meaning of life.

◇◇◇◇◇

THOUGH I'VE SPENT many, many evenings watching foxes, only a fraction of that time was spent taking pictures. That's the price you pay to capture wildlife on camera. But standing in the middle of a deserted Père-Lachaise waiting for them to appear is far from boring. It's an experience in itself. Hearing nothing but silence in the middle of Paris is a luxury that frequently makes me feel like I'm in the countryside. Time seems to pass differently when you're lying in wait. The minutes are longer, slower, and more peaceful, which offsets the frantic pace of my workdays. I listen to nature. I train my eye to the stillness of the tombstones. I watch for the slightest sign of my furry friends. I listen to the rustle of leaves and the twitter of birds. I breathe in and out, perfectly relaxed. I'm enveloped by calm. Nothing else matters.

WATCHING THE BABY FOXES grow up inside the cemetery and witnessing so much of their lives—even just catching their eye—has made me very attached to them. I was quite distraught when I came across the lifeless body of one cub sprawled across a tomb, as if it had died in its sleep. Although I learned that foxes have a high mortality rate in their first year of life, the sight pained me. It was the smallest of the litter and had probably succumbed to natural selection. But the episode was a reality check; it reminded me that while the foxes of Père-Lachaise have an irresistible charm, they are nonetheless wild animals fighting for survival on a daily basis.

Beyond my affection for them, I've often wondered if they've grown used to my presence, or if they even recognize me. Especially the mother of the litter born in 2021. I think I could pick her out of a thousand others: bright-red fur, round eyes, a wide face, big ears with rounded tips. I admire the strength and courage it takes to raise her cubs in a place like Père-Lachaise. On more than one occasion, she posed in front of my lens with the unstudied elegance of a Hollywood starlet. One evening, after leaving her pups with some prey, she started toward me. For a moment, her eyes stared straight into mine, unblinking. Then, only feet from where I stood, she calmly turned and trotted off toward her favorite hunting ground. That evening, I didn't have the impression she saw me as a threat. It might just be my confirmation bias speaking, but I like to think that she recognizes me, that she knows I live in the cemetery, too, that I'm also raising my kids here, and that my name is Benoît (this last point may be a stretch, I admit). Even so, I'm not looking to get closer to the foxes. I don't want to pet or cuddle them in the middle of the cemetery. Our relationship must remain tenuous. Their fear of humans is, in my eyes, a fundamental part of what makes them wild and ensures their survival. They're predators; they should never be fed. As curator, my role mustn't go beyond managing the cemetery in a way that respects their natural habitat so they can continue to live and reproduce among the graves.

Although I was delighted to come across foxes living in Père-Lachaise, the news could have caused a stir. Foxes tend to have a bad reputation, and marveling at wild animals frolicking across headstones might have seemed inappropriate, like a flagrant lack of respect for the dead. But so far, nobody has complained. Quite the opposite, in fact. I've received lots of messages from families thanking me for the photos. They report being reassured and moved by the presence of these animals so near to their loved ones. Some even express hope that the foxes will sleep on their graves and keep them company. These are the most touching letters I've received. In fact, it isn't unusual for visitors, even those mourning a loss, to ask after the foxes, as if they, too, had grown fond of them. I remember selling a concession to a woman who'd come to bury her father and how the exchange had been particularly difficult. She'd been very closed-off, which was perfectly understandable given the circumstances. But as she was getting up to leave once the meeting was over, she turned back to me abruptly and asked how the little foxes were doing. After I assured her they were quite well, she said she was glad her father would be laid to rest in a place where they lived. For the first time that day, I saw her face break into a smile.

Time to Celebrate

I**N FRANCE AND** around the world, All Saints' Day is a public holiday observed on November 1 that is associated with commemorating the dead. It's a very busy day for cemeteries. Still, it falls during an unpopular time of year. The days get shorter, the temperature drops, and the trees lose their leaves. The world withdraws into itself. Only children seem to enjoy the half-light of autumn that with Halloween gives them an excuse to dress up as zombies, vampires, or witches, to carve pumpkins and decorate the house with skulls and fake spiderwebs.

For most adults, the mood is less festive. In France, a country still very attached to honoring the memory of its dead, All Saints' Day is synonymous with cemeteries and chrysanthemums. For some, it's a chore; for others, a pleasure. But if you only go to the cemetery once a year, this is the day. The tradition is a relatively recent one, in fact, which emerged during the nineteenth century as new cemeteries modeled on Père-Lachaise were built. They fostered new customs that revolutionized Parisians' relationship to the dead and reshaped commemorative rites.

This period saw a rise in funeral processions, a tradition that was intended to reflect the deceased's social status. Everything from the church decor to the mass schedule, hearse type, number of horses, and choice of mourning drapes was decided ahead of time. The rich were able to afford a first-class funeral, while the poor were given the bare minimum. It wasn't until the 1970s that customs began to change. Today, even wealthy families no longer feel the need to mark the occasion with great pageantry.

No matter how families choose to honor their dead nowadays, it's typically only the loved ones who accompany the body to its final resting place inside the cemetery. This wasn't always the case, however. In the early days of Père-Lachaise, celebrity funerals sometimes drew large crowds. People would line up to hear leading figures deliver the eulogy, such as Victor Hugo for his friend Balzac: "Gentlemen, the man who now goes down into this tomb is one of those to whom public grief pays homage."[3]

Over time, the French got into the habit of returning to the cemetery to visit the graves of their loved ones. These outings usually take place on a Sunday, when visitors plant flowers, clean the gravestone, or lay a memorial wreath. Performing these rituals would become an integral part of the grieving process.

Starting in the 1850s, All Souls' Day, on November 2, became the culmination of this new relationship with the dead. Although the holiday had been included in the Catholic calendar as early as 998, it had previously only been marked by religious services. Now, All Souls' Day offered the French a reason to pay respects to their dead by decorating their graves with flowers and candles. But since the federal holiday fell on All Saints' Day—the day before All Souls' Day—the celebrations migrated, and November 1 became

Chrysanthemums: The funeral flower?

In France, chrysanthemums are strongly associated with death and mourning. They are such a somber flower, in fact, that offering mums on a social occasion would be considered a big faux pas! How did these cheerful, hardy plants commonly associated with the fall harvest elsewhere in the world become such a symbol of grief?

To commemorate the first anniversary of the World War I Armistice on November 11, 1919, French president Raymond Poincaré ordered the tombs of fallen soldiers to be decorated with flowers. The French people embraced the idea and adopted the chrysanthemum, chosen primarily because its bloom season coincided with the date. The tradition would later extend to all tombs, not just those belonging to soldiers, making chrysanthemums the unofficial emblem of cemeteries.

the most visited day of the year. As a growing number of people started to observe the occasion, media outlets began publishing Parisian cemeteries' attendance records in their November 3 edition.

The tradition proved a lasting one: November 1 is still unquestionably the biggest day of the year at Père-Lachaise. Fifty thousand people walked through its gates in 2015—a figure unequaled since. This may seem like an impressive number, but it's nothing compared to the turn of the twentieth century, when administrative records logged close to 100,000 visitors! Today, many families stretch their visits out over several weeks in order to see loved ones scattered across multiple cemeteries. Pilgrimages to tidy the graves and plant chrysanthemums usually begin in mid-October and can last through mid-November.

For the City of Paris Division of Cemeteries, All Saints' Day is the equivalent of Christmas for toy stores or Easter for chocolate shops. The biggest difference is that we aren't selling anything; we're offering a meaningful public service to visitors, most of whom only come on this occasion.

◇◇◇◇◇

PREPARATIONS BEGIN in September. Everyone sits down together: the division head, deputy division head, cemetery curators, and support staff. The goal is to identify every need so that we can be ready to welcome families under the best conditions. It's when we go over the dates for planting beds of chrysanthemums, vehicle rentals to transport guests, overtime hours to keep the office open, content for new signage, the number of additional maintenance workers and personnel needed, and more.

No matter how much we prepare so that everything runs smoothly, the problem remains the same each year: All Saints' Day happens in the fall. To be sure, Père-Lachaise is at its most beautiful; the shades of red, orange, yellow, gold, and crimson are a feast for the eyes. But it's also the moment when the leaves are falling fastest, which poses its share of problems for a site that has over four thousand trees. Lining the ground and covering paths, fallen leaves hide uneven ground, increasing the risk of falling and slowing us down. If not picked up, they can also give the impression the cemetery isn't well maintained. And yet, the groundskeepers work six days a week beginning in late September to pick up as much as possible and clear the cemetery's main boulevards. It's a tough, thankless job, and they often feel stuck in a time loop, doomed to relive the same day over and over like Bill Murray in *Groundhog Day.* Paths cleared the day before are immediately covered with a new carpet of leaves that must be raked. As a result of their efforts, 150,000 cubic feet of green waste are removed from the cemetery each year.

But that doesn't stop the complaints. Some people seem to forget that leaves fall in autumn and describe the cemetery as "very dirty." Despite my best efforts to explain our limitations, arguing that the myriad benefits of trees outweigh the inconvenience of falling leaves, I get the impression some hardliners wish a groundskeeper with a net would stand under each tree to catch the leaves as they fall.

TIME TO CELEBRATE

WHEN NOVEMBER 1 finally arrives, the excitement is palpable among staff members, who are suddenly happy to work on a public holiday. The cemetery is packed from the moment the gates open. All security guards are on hand to support and direct the families rushing about with their potted chrysanthemums. Informational signs are posted at each entrance to display the holiday policy and remind patrons to renew their concession, if need be. The cemetery is closed to vehicles due to the high volume of visitors, but free shuttles are available for people with mobility issues. This much-appreciated service is provided by the gravediggers, who are happy to transport the living for a change.

The administrative office is open all day so staff can answer any questions visitors might have. How many spaces are left in my family plot? Will I be able to be buried there? Is it possible to buy a plot ahead of time? How do I renew my concession? Can urns be stored in the vault? How do remains transfers work? Can I bury my cat's urn next to my mother-in-law? The list goes on.

Many visitors also come to ask, rather sheepishly, if we can direct them to their plot, explaining that they can't manage to find it given the size of the site. The staff, ever gracious, are quick to acknowledge that the cemetery's sprawling grounds and tangle of paths can be difficult to navigate. Some come to the wrong cemetery entirely, convinced that their loved one is interred at Père-Lachaise when our database indicates they're buried in Montmartre. To be fair, the two cemeteries do resemble each other.

Occasionally, families can't find their plot because it simply doesn't exist anymore; the administration has taken back the land. These are the moments our staff dread the most. It's never easy to break the bad news, to explain the concession wasn't renewed on time or that it was repossessed on grounds of abandonment. Trickier still is explaining that the remains have been exhumed and placed in a small container called a reliquary, which now sits in the ossuary. Families, shocked to learn they've lost their loved ones for a second time, usually react with anger, guilt, and bitterness. What

"To the dead"

The *Monument to the Dead*, by sculptor Albert Bartholomé, honors the memory of people whose remains are unidentified or missing, as well as those who never had or have since lost their graves. Built into the Charonne hill, located a straight shot from the main entrance and just below the East Chapel, this monument, unusual even for its time, was inaugurated with great fanfare on November 1, 1899. It is a secular memorial dedicated to the memory of all those who have died, without distinction. It depicts a couple, seen from the back, as they walk toward a doorway symbolizing the afterlife while their fellow mortals look on in despair at the inexorable fate that awaits them. It's a perfect representation of humanity's anguish in the face of the unknown. Bartholomé himself was laid to rest in a tomb beside his masterpiece.

they thought would be the deceased's last earthly home was, in fact, their second-to-last. Sometimes, when guests fail to grasp the situation, I have to step in. I give the same explanation—almost word for word—as my colleagues, but it usually helps to defuse the tension. We remind families that there is a place in Père-Lachaise where they can continue to pay their respects and lay flowers: the elaborate *Monument to the Dead*, dedicated to anyone who doesn't have a grave of their own.

Behind the monument is a little-known ossuary, accessible through the doors on either side, that opened in 1953. Until 2008, it held the bones of Parisians relocated from the city's fourteen cemeteries; in January 2009, it also began receiving remains relocated from concessions at the six cemeteries outside the city limits. When it reached its capacity in 2014, a new ossuary was opened at Thiais Cemetery.

In the collective imagination, ossuaries are often pictured as giant crypts with bones piled high—a sort of Catacombs 2.0. The Père-Lachaise ossuary is nothing like that. Spread over four levels, its galleries and rooms are stacked with reliquaries that contain the bones of the deceased. Remains are never mixed: each reliquary holds the bones exhumed from a single plot, which lie in the ossuary in perpetuity.

ALL SAINTS' DAY in Père-Lachaise is the only day of the year when grieving families outnumber tourists. It's unusual to have so many mourners in the cemetery at once, and the emotion is unmistakable. On this solemn day full of heartache, I occasionally witness poignant family moments: the grandparents, voices swelling with pride, who tell their grandchildren about the lives of their ancestors as they clean their graves; the widow who, tears in her eyes, touches her hand to her lips and tenderly transfers a kiss to her husband's tomb; the daughter who gently tosses a rose onto the lawn where her father's ashes are scattered. These rituals, in their simplicity and symbolism, share a common purpose: they remind us that the dead and the living belong to the same community.

Finally, you can't have All Saints' Day without its host of seasonal content—all the articles and press reports that tend to recycle the same material year after year: the price tag of a funeral, a report on shady funeral directors, an exposé on overcrowded cemeteries, a feature on chrysanthemums, and all the rest. Some outlets try for a more original angle, deciding instead to run articles on green burials or cemeteries in the digital age. Others publish Halloween-themed articles about the supernatural or an interview with a "vampirologist" to showcase the cemetery's hidden symbols. It's harmless, really; Père-Lachaise is brimming with legends of all kinds. The problem is that some people believe them. One All Saints' Day, someone came to the office to ask where he could find the tomb of Vlad Țepeș, "also known as Vlad the Impaler," he added earnestly. We were very sorry to have to tell him that, despite what he might have read or heard on TV, Dracula wasn't buried in Père-Lachaise.

But even if it means wandering the cemetery until dusk, the one grave you shouldn't miss is that of Frédéric Chopin. Every November 1, it stands out from all the rest. Instead of chrysanthemums, dozens of candles honor the late composer in the Polish tradition. At sundown, right before the cemetery closes, the tomb illuminated by countless flickering lights is a thing of beauty.

◇◇◇◇◇

ALL SAINTS' DAY falls during an unpopular time of year. And yet, this period traditionally reserved for mourning the dead is my favorite time of year. I look forward to it, and I wouldn't miss it for anything in the world. It's such an important occasion that in the small circle of death care professionals, experience is counted in November firsts and not in years.

I have nineteen under my belt, and I can't wait for the next.

Living Among the Dead

I F WORKING IN a cemetery is rather unusual, living in one is even more so. Yet this is what I've been doing ever since I became a curator.

Parisian cemeteries are vast, heavily trafficked spaces and are one of the rare municipal services open every day. As a result, the curators who manage them must be readily available to address all requests. They can be called on at any moment, including weekends and holidays, if an emergency arises. For this reason, curators are usually housed on site in order to carry out their duties.

Personally, living in a cemetery has never fazed me. Given my family history, I wasn't too worried—quite the opposite, really. The thought of returning to my childhood universe enchanted me. There were practical advantages, too: no more taking public transit to work. My eldest son was excited to trade our old apartment for a new one with a big yard. My wife was a different story. She was happy for me when I told her I'd gotten the job at Père-Lachaise, but once I announced we'd be living in a staff apartment on the grounds, her enthusiasm dwindled. Living alongside the dead didn't appeal to her; unlike me, she wasn't lucky enough to have grown up with a yard scattered with tombstones. But despite her initial objections, and after a few sleepless nights, she got used to our new surroundings. In truth, when we're inside the apartment, we forget about the thousands of graves on the other side of the wall. My wife adapted so well, in fact, that she ended up leaving the restaurant business and pivoted to... the funeral business! With my encouragement (and a few gentle nudges), she took the plunge and gave the industry a try. I knew she would make an excellent funeral consultant, and I was right. She's thriving, despite daily contact with grieving families. And to think, she never would have discovered the profession had life not thrown me into her path...

◇◇◇◇◇

EVEN THOUGH WE'VE become known as the "Addams Family," neither our jobs nor the fact that we live inside a cemetery has made us sad, let alone depressed. Unlike our lifeless neighbors, we're determined to live life to the fullest. Since we've been living among the dead, we've logged a wedding and numerous trips and have helped to grow France's population: three of our children were born between 2011 and 2019, none of whom has lived anywhere other than a cemetery. They took their first steps among the graves and learned to ride bicycles along tomb-lined boulevards. Like me, my four children are growing up in a world where death is omnipresent. Like me, they seem entirely unbothered by it. They think Père-Lachaise is a funny place filled with famous people, lots of tourists, and cute foxes, but they're reluctant to spend time there; they much prefer the nearby playgrounds of Square de la Roquette or Jardin Casque-d'Or. As parents, that suits us just fine. The important thing is that they don't feel uncomfortable growing up in a cemetery or having two parents who work in the funeral industry. They don't seem to mind, and so far, they haven't taken us to court.

◇◇◇◇◇

ALTHOUGH WE'RE USED to living among the dead, our situation can surprise, and even unsettle, people unfamiliar with our family. One September, my daughter told her new teacher that her house was in Père-Lachaise. The teacher hadn't believed her; she assumed Rose had problems with spatial awareness and that we, like a number of her classmates, probably lived in an apartment that overlooked the cemetery. When Rose insisted, the teacher contacted me, and I confirmed that my daughter wasn't a pathological liar—that we did, in fact, live in a staff apartment inside the cemetery. She laughed at her mistake and admitted that she didn't know that was possible. A few months later, for the first time in her career, she took her class on a field trip to Père-Lachaise. Rose was delighted.

We want our children to have a fairly normal social life, so we host their birthday parties in our apartment every year. When it comes to the invitations, writing our address always gives us pause: should we note that we live inside Père-Lachaise and risk scaring guests? Or should we write "16, Rue du Repos" and risk coming off as strange when parents learn this is the cemetery's official address? Whatever we decide, there's always a moment when we have to explain the party will take place inside a cemetery. No picnics or treasure hunts between the tombs; just a run-of-the-mill birthday party in our staff apartment. Once they get past their astonishment, most parents find our living arrangements to be quirky, even entertaining, and gladly entrust their children to us.

◇◇◇◇◇

I DON'T KNOW if my children will ever realize how lucky they are to have grown up in a cemetery—particularly in Père-Lachaise. How will it influence their lives? Perhaps they'll be unaffected by such close contact with the dead. Or perhaps it will have an impact, even subconsciously, on their personalities. It's impossible to say.

What I *can* say is that during the first lockdown, in spring 2020, they were luckier than their Parisian classmates. The cemetery was closed to the public, so my children had the run of all 110 acres. Because the weather was so nice, each weekend our family would go sit on the benches in front of the East Chapel to bask in the sun and admire the stunning view of the Eiffel Tower. Despite the apocalyptic mood that had settled over a subdued Paris, we were keenly aware of our luck. Every weekday, while I worked, my wife would take the children on long, winding walks through the cemetery's deserted paths. Over time, they developed a favorite route that included the bucolic Chemin des Chèvres and two graves they'd grown particularly fond of. The first belonged to singer Gilbert Bécaud, France's "Monsieur 100,000 Volts," whose tomb was decorated with a little blue piano at the time. The second was the grave of three-year-old Arnaud, which had made an impression on them. They liked dropping by to say hi on their daily walks. Within a few weeks, "We're going for a walk" became "We're going to see Gilbert and Arnaud." It was our little code. My children will forever associate these graves with the pandemic, and I'm convinced that one day when they tell their grandchildren about the lockdowns, they'll talk about Gilbert and Arnaud.

During the first lockdown, I also asked my children to take pictures of any spaces they came across where there was no sign of a grave. You never know, I figured. With a bit of luck, they might find an available plot or two. The children know that space in the cemetery is scarce, and they were so amused by the hunt that they didn't even realize I was getting free labor out of them. They saw it as a game, like a giant, real-life *Where's Waldo?*, except that instead of a man in a red-and-white-striped shirt, they were searching for an empty plot among thousands.

In the evenings, I checked the status of the unmarked spaces they found in the cemetery records; in most cases they were already spoken for, conceded in perpetuity. One day, however, I was pleasantly surprised. A patch of land located inside the historically Muslim section of Division 85, an area I thought had been full for some time, was free. I'd found a new plot! In an unbelievable coincidence, the Kabyle singer Idir died days later, on May 2, 2020, and his relatives called to ask whether there was a concession available in this section. Naturally, I offered it to them—although

How many bodies are buried in Père-Lachaise?

Thousands of bodies have been buried in the cemetery since it first opened in 1804. According to burial records, which are now available to the public on the Archives de Paris website, it wasn't unusual for thirty or forty bodies to be buried in Père-Lachaise each day.

Some were interred in common graves; others in individual free plots, columbarium niches, or family concessions. Still others were scattered on the Memorial Garden or transferred to other Parisian cemeteries, only to end up back in Père-Lachaise's ossuary between 1953 and 2014 (when it was closed for lack of space).

With all of these categories combined, the number of bodies in Père-Lachaise today is estimated at around 1.3 million. Given that not all of the 220 years of archives have been digitized, this figure is an extrapolation based on office records and historical data.

I had to point out that most of the graves currently occupying the space aren't Muslim, and that cemeteries have been officially secular since 1881. The Algerian musician was buried in Père-Lachaise on May 13, 2020. The last time a concession had been granted in that section was in 1993. Thanks to my children, Idir is now there too.

◇◇◇◇◇

I CAN SEE how living among the dead might be a frightening prospect. The least inclined tell me the idea of being surrounded by hundreds of thousands of corpses spooks them. Others would be willing to pay good money to spend a night among the dead, but Père-Lachaise doesn't offer Airbnb-type packages—at least not yet. And not to disappoint the horror-movie buffs out there, but I've never come across zombies or vampires in either of the cemeteries I've lived in. Incredibly, my birthday is October 31, the day of Halloween—you can't make this stuff up—but I've got nothing to show for it. I've never even spotted a will-o'-the-wisp. And that's not for lack of roaming around cemeteries, sometimes very late at night.

Unsurprisingly, nights in Père-Lachaise are very calm; everything is, as you might expect, deathly still. Whenever there's a full moon, or if a cloud traps light from the city, the cemetery is bathed in a pale-orange glow. Once your eyes have adjusted to the dim light, you can wander around without so much as a flashlight. Though it sounds eerie, it's actually very peaceful. For a moment, it feels like you're in the quietest spot in Paris.

But when there's no moon, the ambiance is very different—and not nearly as peaceful. On these nights, my ears perk up at the slightest rustle and my imagination can easily run wild. Reason gives way to emotion, and in a strange role reversal, it can suddenly feel as if the statues are watching my every move. Although I can scarcely make them out in the darkness, I feel their eyes on me. Their presence is suffocating. As someone who doesn't believe in the paranormal and who generally scoffs at any mention of ghosts or spirits, I have to admit that a pitch-black cemetery makes me uneasy. It feels as though I'm angering the dead, who were hoping for a quiet night after spending the day trampled by tourists. I have a sudden urge to keep my head down and pick up the pace, fearing, perhaps, that I'll be spotted by a tuxedoed figure determined to sink his teeth into my neck. Yet reason eventually wins out. The sensation of being watched slowly fades, as if the dead have sunk back into their eternal slumber after briefly waking to see who dares to wander alone at night through their domain. While I've always returned safe and sound, I'm not a fan of these nocturnal outings. I only go out at night when necessary, either for professional reasons or to set up my motion detection camera to capture videos of animals using night vision.

◇◇◇◇◇

ALL THINGS CONSIDERED, I enjoy having the dead for neighbors. They are discreet tenants who never cause nighttime disturbances, never come by at inopportune moments to borrow an egg or a cup of flour, and never leave nasty messages in the elevator. While some of the more famous residents receive scores of visitors during the day, a profound silence always settles over their resting places by night. What's more, they never complain about how noisy my children are or tell me to turn the music down when we throw parties.

As you can see, I'm in no hurry to get back to living among the living.

Ghost Stories

"IS IT TRUE? Do you really keep Oscar Wilde's balls on your desk?" This is probably one of the most unexpected questions I've ever been asked, although it comes up every so often due to a legend involving the famous Irish writer's grave. The question isn't referring to the genitals of Oscar Wilde himself, but to those of the sphinx that adorns his tomb. Designed by the American sculptor Jacob Epstein, the "flying demon-angel" caused a scandal when it was unveiled at Père-Lachaise in 1912. The unconventional nude on display provoked such public outcry that the prefect ordered it to be covered with a tarpaulin until its fate could be decided and tempers calmed. On October 25, 1912, members of the prefecture of the former Seine department's Ethics and Aesthetics Committee described the work as "bizarre... unattractive and of dubious taste." The outrage specifically targeted the sphinx's genitals, which some considered inappropriate for a cemetery. Depicting a nude was a bold move for the time, even though Wilde, with his reputation for scandal, would likely have been no stranger to the furor his funeral monument sparked.

The sphinx's stone testicles were allegedly removed by two English women visiting Paris who were appalled by the sculpture. Yet official cemetery records make no mention of these overzealous puritans. Only a notarized staff report dated September 12, 1961, mentions that "the testicles on Oscar Wilde's monument have been damaged by an unknown person." Ever since, countless articles about Père-Lachaise have claimed that the genitals were recovered by cemetery employees and have been used as a paperweight by successive curators. Naturally, when I began my new job, I searched every filing cabinet and combed through the paperwork my predecessor had left me. Alas, I found nothing; there was no trace of the "relic." Even today, journalists or fans of Père-Lachaise still ask me about the defaced monument—so often that I must frequently deny keeping the stone testicles on my desk.

This anecdote is a perfect example of what makes Père-Lachaise unusual beyond its landscaping and rich heritage. The cemetery's untold legends give it a certain aura and feed its international reputation. The stories come in all shapes and sizes, covering old and new ground alike, each more bizarre than the last. But together, they make Père-Lachaise a fascinating and intriguing place in the heart of Paris.

SOME PEOPLE CLAIM that Père-Lachaise is the most haunted spot in the city, a place of witchcraft and satanic worship. Black masses are still said to be practiced, a myth many gullible people believe to this day. In reality, Père-Lachaise hasn't been the site of occult rituals in years—if ever. While it's true that many defiled monuments bear the scars of satanic rites, these likely occurred in the 1970s and '80s, when the cemetery allegedly had a thriving nightlife.

No, there's no trace of Satan or Lucifer in Père-Lachaise. No, Marshal Kellermann, Duke of Valmy, isn't the devil, even if his plot bears the number 666. No, Dracula isn't buried in the Leduc chapel. No, there are no secret entrances leading to the Catacombs, the Élysée Palace, or directly to Hell...

The only strange thing I've seen was hundreds of sacrificial chickens found in the vault of a concession the City had recently repossessed. Cemetery gravediggers had to remove twenty square feet of dead birds before they could get to the bodies. The bizarre discovery was likely the work of one individual who stuffed the birds through a crack in the abandoned grave after performing a voodoo ritual.

Another fun fact is that I regularly receive official correspondence from ghost-hunting societies requesting permission to visit the cemetery at night with their equipment (spirit boxes, electromagnetic field sensors, Ouija boards, etc.) to check for paranormal activity. Though I'm a fan of the *Ghostbusters* movies, I have to tell them they can't hunt ghosts in the middle of the cemetery.

For those who sincerely believe the place is teeming with apparitions and spirits, let's be clear: these legends were probably invented and perpetuated by guides in order to develop a clientele of thrill-seekers.

◇◇◇◇

THERE ARE ALSO stories linking Père-Lachaise to people who are still very much alive. Legend has it that before Andreï Makine became a famous writer and member of the Académie française, he used to live in a cemetery vault.

Bestselling novelist Amélie Nothomb is rumored to be a cemetery regular; I've lost count of the number of people who have told me they ran into her. I've never seen her personally,

Perpetual concessions: Myth or reality?

The French funeral industry is full of myths. The most common one I hear is that perpetual concessions no longer exist, or that their duration is actually limited to ninety-nine years. So let me set the record straight.

Perpetual concessions are one of four types of funeral concessions established under French law. Municipalities still have the option to grant perpetual concessions, but many prefer to issue "temporary" (defined as up to fifteen years), thirty-, or fifty-year concessions to simplify administrative procedures. Perpetual concessions were the only type available at Père-Lachaise until 2003; today, they still represent 92 percent of all of the cemetery's concessions. Contrary to popular belief, these really do last forever. The oldest concession and I tend to think her frequent presence in Père-Lachaise, like a wandering ghost, is just a myth that surrounds the mysterious writer. The only visible trace of her is the inscription "Amélie Nothomb Bar" etched into the altar of a neo-Gothic chapel located on Chemin de la Cave. "Cellar Street"—it pairs perfectly with her love of champagne.

Finally, there are myths associated with residents who aren't famous but whose graves are among the most visited because of the supernatural powers they're rumored to possess. With its multitude of decrepit tombstones, macabre symbolism, and dense vegetation, the cemetery's

in the cemetery dates back to 1804, the year the cemetery opened.

Perpetual concessions that fall into disrepair after their families have stopped maintaining them can look unsightly and affect a cemetery's ability to function properly. To address these concerns, a 1924 law allows municipalities to repossess concessions declared "abandoned." In this case, that means any outward signs of neglect (cracks or shifts in the foundation, gaps that leave the interior of the vault exposed, crumbling headstones, overgrown weeds, etc.). A lack of beneficiaries or a flowerless tombstone does not constitute abandonment. Through these administrative channels, a handful of plots become available each year to Parisian families.

unique atmosphere no doubt contributes to the profusion of myths that are impossible to dispel. Ambling through Père-Lachaise, it feels as though time doesn't exist and the outside world has no hold over you. In these moments, it's easy to let your imagination run wild.

While I'm fairly down-to-earth, I was amazed to discover that Père-Lachaise is a popular spot among fans of esotericism, Spiritism, myths, mysteries, magic, and the occult. I'm constantly surrounded by these myths and legends. They follow me everywhere and are impossible to escape. It doesn't matter whether I think they're fascinating or a tourist trap; they're part and parcel of my job. They're a piece of the cemetery's intangible heritage, a feature that is just as important as its chapels, celebrity graves, and hundred-year-old trees. Together, they add to its charm.

The myths and legends tied to Père-Lachaise are as numerous as they are diverse. I don't claim to know them all, but I can list a few of the main attractions that have become popular shrines.

Are you struggling with one issue in particular? Whatever your trouble, there's bound to be a grave somewhere in the cemetery that can help you solve your problem.

◇◇◇◇

UNLUCKY IN LOVE? Place an ace of hearts on the tomb of Mademoiselle Lenormand, fortune teller to the rich and famous, and let her divine your path to romance. Some also say her grave has the power to recharge tarot cards left by aspiring clairvoyants during a full moon.

NOT SEEING STRAIGHT? Late Spiritist Rufina Noeggerath, known as Bonne Maman, should be able to help. Legend has it her grave can cure vision problems—just take a leaf from one of the plants in her plot and rub it over your eyes.

MONEY PROBLEMS? The towering mausoleum of Baroness Demidoff, laid to rest in Père-Lachaise in 1818, can help you strike it rich. Beginning around 1889, reports from Belgium, the United States, Australia, and Great Britain claimed that an immensely wealthy Russian woman had left two million rubles in her will to anyone who managed to spend an entire year in the crypt alongside her body. The rules allegedly prohibited contact with the outside world and limited outings to an hour each day before the cemetery gates opened. Though Uber Eats hadn't been invented yet, the articles stated that meals were to be delivered daily and left at the vault door. It may have seemed an easy challenge for misanthropes who liked to read and had little regard for food, but there was a catch: the baroness was said to rest in a crystal coffin, making her decomposing body visible. Interested parties were to address applications to Paris City Hall.

My predecessors received applications from all over the world, some of which are still on file at the Archives de Paris. The news articles don't mention baroness Demidoff by name, but since she came from a wealthy family of Russian industrialists, some quickly connected her to the massive tomb adorned with wolf heads, sables, and hammers. These were a nod to the metalworking and fur trade industries, sources of the family fortune. It should be noted that the same legend is also linked to the grave of Ms. Dias-Santos, a young woman who died in 1827 at the age of sixteen and whose unusual grave lies at the foot of Félix de Beaujour's immense lighthouse-shaped tomb. The last foreign articles to mention the legend reference the tomb of a certain Ruth Curtis, whose name doesn't appear in any of the cemetery registers.

Of course, none of it is real—not the will or the crystal casket. Don't bother sending an application; it'll just end up in the trash. The whole story was probably fabricated by the press at a time when competition between newspapers was fierce and before journalists followed a code of ethics. It's a good example of a canard: a misleading story that aims to deceive. This hoax became an urban legend that sailed around the world and still fascinates to this day. Though I no longer receive hundreds of letters like my predecessors did at the end of the nineteenth century, I have received two applications from abroad so far, more than a century after the legend was born.

FERTILITY ISSUES? If you're a fan of the erotic, then head to Victor Noir's grave. Killed at only twenty-one on January 10, 1870, by Pierre Bonaparte, a cousin of Napoleon III, the young journalist played a pivotal role in France's history. His murder effectively reinforced hostility toward the Second Empire, which would soon be overthrown, paving the way for the Third Republic. A cult following developed around Victor Noir, considered by revolutionaries to be a victim of imperial policy and a martyr to the republican cause. Initially buried in Neuilly-sur-Seine, his remains were transferred to Père-Lachaise under pressure from the public. To mark the occasion, a recumbent bronze statue designed by Jules Dalou was financed by a national subscription and erected in his memory. Victor Noir's tomb is regularly included on guided tours or in tributes to figures of the Paris Commune, but today it's best known due to a strange superstition: rubbing the statue's genitals is said to enhance fertility. Once seen as a political symbol, today Victor Noir is a sex symbol.

His grave is one of the cemetery's most popular. Every day, tourists snap pictures of themselves touching the statue's crotch, most of them unaware of the role its model played in history. In 2004, the City of Paris attempted to curb the horseplay by putting up fencing around the tomb. In vain.

If you look at the statue, you'll see the verdigris has been rubbed away not only from the crotch but from other parts of the body as well. Apparently, Victor Noir was a man of many talents. Touching his feet will lead you to the love of your life, and kissing his lips, nose, or chin, or placing a finger over the spot where the bullet pierced his heart, will bring back a wayward love. Some individuals or couples perform these rituals very seriously, hoping their wish will come true. They leave flowers in his hat or messages on scraps of paper, either to beg for his help or to thank him.

A WISH YOU'D LIKE GRANTED? You won't want to miss the grave of Hippolyte Léon Denizard Rivail. The name doesn't ring a bell? Don't worry, you're not alone. He is Père-Lachaise's most famous resident nobody's ever heard of, and his grave is one of the most visited in the cemetery.

As Rivail was leading a quiet life in Paris as a teacher and educational writer, a new practice imported from the United States known as table-turning was growing in popularity. It wasn't until 1855, at the ripe age of fifty-one, that the tables began to turn—no pun intended—for Rivail. After a friend invited him to a séance, he left the experience a convert. He began participating in table-turning sessions one after the other, which enabled him to make contact with several different spirits. One of these spirits, Zephyr, told him they'd met previously in another life, when both men were living in ancient Gaul. He added, "We were friends. You were a druid, and your name was Allan Kardec."

From then on, Hippolyte Rivail became known as Allan Kardec. He published several works on Spiritism under the same name, including his most famous *The Spirits' Book* in 1857. After that, his life would never be the same. The book was very accessible—remember, he'd been a teacher—and was an instant hit. Like all religions, Kardec's Spiritism contains dogmas, including the most important: reincarnation. This belief holds that spirits who communicate with the living are waiting for a new body to begin a new life. Kardec's teachings sparked a huge following across France, where he gave lectures to enthusiastic audiences. After all, who doesn't want to believe that it's possible to talk to the dead and come back to life after you die?

Kardec's late calling as a Spiritist came to an abrupt end on March 31, 1869, when he died of a ruptured aneurysm. He was buried at Montmartre Cemetery and transferred to

Père-Lachaise on March 29, 1879, where his remains lie in a granite tomb shaped like a dolmen. Shortly before he died, Allan Kardec allegedly declared, "After my death, if you come to see me, place a hand on the neck of the statue that will overlook my tomb, then make a wish. If your wish is granted, come back with flowers." What a clever guy, that Allan! In addition to being one of the most visited graves in the cemetery, his is also one of the most colorful.

◇◇◇◇◇

WHO SAID CEMETERIES were depressing? Thanks to its legends, it's possible to walk out of Père-Lachaise reinvigorated and full of hope.

Under the Parisian Sky

PÈRE-LACHAISE IS HOME to one extraordinary songbird that is second to none. I'm speaking, of course, of Édith Giovanna Gassion, nicknamed *la Môme Piaf* ("Little Sparrow") in her early years by Louis Leplée, the first cabaret manager to hire her, for her petite frame and unparalleled voice. After rising to international stardom for recording what would become some of France's most popular hits, Édith Piaf passed away on October 10, 1963. Along with Frédéric Chopin and Jim Morrison, she is one of the cemetery's most visited celebrities. Even foreign tourists flock to her modest tomb like pigeons to a crust of bread.

Yet if you go beyond Division 97 where the icon of French chanson rests, and if you raise your head and listen carefully, you'll catch a glimpse of other little sparrows of all kinds. Each year, around sixty different species can be spotted in Père-Lachaise. Of these, only twenty or so nest in the cemetery—the others are just passing through or taking a break along their migration route. But the number gives some indication of the variety of birds that can be identified with a pair of good binoculars. Père-Lachaise: a top-notch ornithological reserve in the heart of Paris!

Crows are the dominant species in the cemetery. They're frequently confused with ravens, which do not live in Paris. Because crows are the only birds that are all black—from their feathers, eyes, and beaks down to their feet—they have a reputation for being birds of ill omen. They're considered to be pests and are hunted throughout the rest of France. That isn't the case here, where their black plumage is perfectly suited to the cemetery's ambiance. Catching sight of a crow perched atop a memorial cross is hardly surprising—in fact, it's almost cliché. Regardless of the superstitions associated with them, Parisian crows have found an ideal refuge in Père-Lachaise, and they're easy to spot: they're very noisy birds, and they tend to hang in packs. Crows aren't shy, and they'll let you get quite close to them. Some have even been tagged to track their movement as part of a research initiative for the National Museum of Natural History. A number of studies have shown them to be a highly intelligent, adaptable species, a far cry from their reputation as common scavengers.

They do, however, cause their share of headaches. They've been known to ravage the flower beds, which staff gardeners or families have meticulously planted, in search of worms. They also tear open garbage bags to pick through food that tourists throw away. During mating season, they won't hesitate to attack passersby who get too close to their nests, performing what looks like a scene out of Hitchcock's *The Birds* right in the middle of the cemetery. Crows are fearless and will occasionally even chase sparrow hawks around the cemetery. The only two animals that drive them nuts, prompting choruses of cawing, are foxes and tawny owls. The racket can be very loud and startling, even frightening, but it's helped me to locate either the crows or their adversaries on more than one occasion. As you pass by the East Chapel, listen carefully. If you hear something that sounds like an ambulance siren, look up to the trees. You'll realize the sound is coming from none other than a crow. Cemetery regulars and staff have started calling it the "nee-naw bird."

As you continue on through the cemetery, you're likely to hear the shrill chirps of rose-ringed parakeets. As the story goes, they managed to escape from a container at Orly Airport about forty years ago and have been a mainstay of Parisian parks, gardens, and cemeteries—including Père-Lachaise—ever since. They can be found near the Gambetta entrance and in the sector by Molière and La Fontaine, as well as close to Abelard and Heloise. They nest all year round in hollow trees, often squatting in abandoned woodpecker holes. With their bright-green plumage and black-and-pink neck rings for males, parakeets are a pretty sight as they flit through the trees, very often in groups. (Note that they never land on the ground.) Their screeching frequently disrupts the solemnity of funerals, distracting guests during a somber moment.

Along your walk, you'll easily be able to spot other, less conspicuous species that live in Père-Lachaise. First, there are a great many woodpeckers (green, spotted, or lesser spotted). If you see a bird flying in an undulating pattern, there's a good chance it's a woodpecker. The sound of them drumming on a hollow tree instantly transports you to the forest. It also helps you spot them, though they can be difficult to see through the foliage and tend to fly away quickly. Careful—they're easily frightened!

There are a number of pigeons (stock doves, rock doves, and wood pigeons), though not nearly as many as in the streets of Paris. The pigeons of Père-Lachaise are attractive birds. They aren't crippled or maimed like many of those seen outside the cemetery, which seems to offer a better quality of life than the city center. Unfortunately for them, they've become the prey of choice for the foxes that now live alongside them.

Sizable populations of great tits (see page 4), Eurasian blue tits (page 182), or long-tailed tits can be seen in the cemetery year-round. Smaller than pigeons, these species have best adapted to living in a cemetery; they won't hesitate to nest in statues or funeral chapels or take baths in the still water that collects on a marble vault cover.

Eurasian magpies are also easy to identify thanks to their characteristic black-and-white plumage. They're relatively rare, however, and I'm inclined to think they purposefully keep their distance from Père-Lachaise and the tomb of Gioachino Rossini, whose opera *The Thieving Magpie* gave them a bad name. Although the remains of the Italian composer have been transferred elsewhere, the Rossini chapel on the main avenue still houses the body of his wife.

As for the chaffinches, though they're not thieves, they are very greedy. They travel in groups and can easily be spotted foraging for food. In my pictures, they're always holding something in their beaks. Their call involves a series of loud *pink* or *chink* sounds, which helps to identify them, but they can also produce more elaborate songs. According to experts, the chaffinch song consists of a bright rattle of notes with a final flourish resembling a *chi chi chi chi chiup chup chup chup too too too wee too*.

No survey of Père-Lachaise's feathered friends would be complete without mentioning blackbirds—and not only because the tomb of Jean-Baptiste Clément, author of "Le Temps des cerises," the revolutionary hymn associated with the Paris Commune, lies opposite the Communards' Wall. "When we sing in cherry season / We hear the blackbird's mocking song…" Although we can hear the blackbird serenade us from its perch in the trees or atop funeral chapels, it isn't to mock us. It's a territorial bird that sings to defend the nest where it lives alone, except during mating season. Opening its bright-orange beak, it trills a warning that means "I'm here!" The colorful beak, which contrasts with the black of its feathers, signals good health and draws the attention of females. Despite its color, the blackbird doesn't fall victim to the same stigma attached to crows or black cats. It stands out thanks to its distinctive song, whose flutelike timbre and rich melodies place the blackbird's voice above all the rest.

The cemetery is home to many other species that can be more difficult to observe, including short-toed treecreepers, Eurasian wrens, common firecrests, Eurasian blackcaps, dunnocks, song thrushes, and black redstarts. Spotting them requires experience, patience, and very often a good pair of binoculars. And let's not forget the birds of prey: Eurasian sparrow hawks, which nest in Père-Lachaise every year, and tawny owls, which I tend not to see but often hear at dusk.

There are also common swifts—birds I never see up close, but whose migration I observe from the cemetery each spring. With an astonishing level of stamina and the ability to sleep in the air, swifts spend most of their lives in the sky. They only land when necessary, primarily to build their nests. Even high up in the sky, they're easy to spot with their slender, crossbow-shaped black wings.

After much time spent observing the many bird species that enjoy Père-Lachaise's bucolic setting, I've developed a fondness for two in particular. The first is the robin, despite its occasionally haughty air. Watching it flit from a bush and land on the rusting gates of an aging tomb is a vision to behold; the red of its breast contrasts magnificently with the headstones. Birds that live in the cemetery tend to be less shy than their countryside counterparts, and robins are no exception. They've been known to pose for the camera, gifting photographers with the perfect photo op and following the rules of modeling to the letter: chin up, neck straight, hold, change poses. And of course, never smile.

The other bird I have a soft spot for is the Eurasian jay (see page 15). Like many Parisians, I wasn't even aware it

existed until I became interested in cemetery wildlife. How could I have missed such a large bird?

I'm not sure why, but I feel a profound connection to the jay, possibly owing to its shyness, which I find touching. Jays are aloof, difficult to approach, and like to hide in the foliage. They aren't as chatty as magpies and don't hang around in groups like crows. They're pretty birds with blue-spotted panels on their wings, and this understated beauty gives them a certain elegance, unlike the flashy green of parakeets.

I like to watch them hunt for acorns among the gravestones. A jay can hold up to seven acorns in its throat pouch, or crop, before burying them underneath moss or leaves in preparation for winter. In so doing, jays, like squirrels, help trees reproduce. In France, they're known as "oak jays" for precisely this reason. Incidentally, jays are also excellent mimics and can imitate sounds in their environment: the meow of a cat, the hoot of an owl, the hiss of a vulture, and more.

The jay's only flaw—nothing's perfect—is its truly awful alarm call, a kind of hoarse, repetitive croak that sounds like a construction vehicle backing up. This call alerts other animals around it, earning the jay the nickname "sentinel of the forest." In the past, this call has helped me spot a tawny owl and several foxes. Maybe that's why I like them.

◆◇◆◇◆

IF SOMEONE HAD told me that I'd develop an interest in birds one day, I never would have believed them—especially since before working and living in a cemetery, I had a very good reason to steer clear: I've been an ornithophobe all my life. To put it simply, I'm afraid of birds. Some people are scared of spiders or mice; for me, it's birds (or really any animal with feathers). It's a phobia few people understand, and it's difficult to come to terms with. Birds aren't particularly frightening, nor do they pose a threat to humans. Saying you're afraid of ducks makes you sound like a chicken. Yet I confess, I'll cross the street at the mere sight of a flock of pigeons. I'm not sure when my phobia first began, possibly back when my grandparents had a farm and I'd go collect eggs from the henhouse. I never really delved deeper, since I've always managed to live with it. Today, taking an interest in the birds that live in the cemetery does more than open my eyes to the world around me and teach me new things. When I photograph them, I'm also learning to conquer an irrational fear. And that's well worth the effort.

Since I'm no stranger to paradoxes, I have another secret to reveal: Édith Piaf isn't the only resident of the cemetery to be named for a bird. My wife, the love of my life, is named Colombe, or "dove" in French. As it turns out, you can be terrified of birds and still love a person named after one.

The Legend of Jim

THE CEMETERY'S most popular celebrity is unquestionably Jim Morrison. After fleeing the United States and dying in Paris at only twenty-seven, the provocative singer was quietly buried in Père-Lachaise. The circumstances surrounding his death are still the subject of much debate. The official story is that Morrison died in his bathtub of heart failure. However, journalist Sam Bernett later claimed that Morrison suffered an overdose in a toilet stall of the Rock'n'Roll Circus, a legendary Parisian nightclub.

Only five people attended his burial in Père-Lachaise, including his girlfriend, Pamela Courson, and their mutual friend Agnès Varda. His grave quickly became a pilgrimage site, attracting fans from around the world. For decades, the public's overzealous devotion to their idol proved a nuisance for successive curators. Fans of The Doors brought the proverbial "sex, drugs, and rock 'n' roll" to life, transforming the Lizard King's grave into a site of hedonism and debauchery. As drug-fueled benders became more common, so did complaints against the addicts, drunks, and derelicts. Junkies would be found lying unconscious between the graves, surrounded by empty bottles and syringes. On May 13, 1981, the Paris bomb squad was called to inspect a grenade found lying beside the tomb, possibly left by a visitor who was outraged by all the unruliness.

To make matters worse, Jim Morrison's grave is quite difficult to access. It's wedged between several other graves in Division 6 and sits just behind a massive funeral chapel, with no direct path to the site. Why this particular location was chosen remains a mystery. Did the curator at the time know who James Douglas Morrison was? Or did the singer's loved ones request that he be buried in a quiet corner of the cemetery? Whatever the case, the neighboring graves have consistently paid the price; they were regularly vandalized, covered in graffiti tributes to the rock star, and used as benches by fans.

Cemetery authorities tried everything to curb the disturbances: implementing round-the-clock security patrols, installing video surveillance, removing graffiti, contacting the U.S. Embassy to see about repatriating Morrison's remains, filing police complaints, and more—to no avail. Jim Morrison is a troublemaker, even in death. In 1991, on the twentieth anniversary of the singer's passing, the cemetery had to call on reinforcements from the CRS, France's riot police, to contain the masses of drunk fans demanding to be let in.

Over time, however, the situation improved. Morrison's grave was assigned a permanent guard. Spike strips and barbed wire were installed along the perimeter walls to deter nighttime intrusions. In 2004, the tomb was finally surrounded by a protective fence. And, don't forget, his fans grew older and wiser.

More than fifty years after his death, Jim Morrison's grave is no longer the site of unrestrained revelry—but it's still the most visited in the cemetery. It is to Père-Lachaise what the *Mona Lisa* is to the Louvre. Tourists flock to Leonardo da Vinci's most famous portrait whether they're aficionados of Renaissance art or not. In the same way, visitors to Père-Lachaise are drawn to Morrison's grave even if they've never heard his lyrics or Ray Manzarek's magnificent keyboard riffs. That's the thing about tourist attractions: they have their own gravitational pull.

◇◇◇◇

MORRISON'S GRAVE CONTINUES to fascinate because of the legends surrounding it. The first concerns a white marble bust sculpted by Croatian artist Mladen Mikulin, which sat on top of the rock icon's grave from May 26, 1981, to May 9, 1988, when it mysteriously disappeared. Many theories explain the theft. According to one, it was stolen by two fans on mopeds who'd hidden out in the cemetery the night before. Another common story claims that staff members recovered the bust, which is still sitting in storage. I can confirm that the latter theory is false: I've looked everywhere, and there's no trace of the bust in a secret location (apart from an unauthorized copy that appeared in the 1990s—the same one that sat in my office in my early days at Père-Lachaise). The fate of the original remains a mystery. Who knows? Maybe it'll turn up one day. Where the bust used to sit, a metal plaque on the tomb now reads: "James Douglas Morrison 1943–1971." Below it, there is an inscription in ancient Greek: ΚΑΤΑ ΤΟΝ ΔΑΙΜΟΝΑ ΕΑΥΤΟΥ, which can be translated as "true to his own demon."

Another legend claims that Jim Morrison is no longer buried in Père-Lachaise. I'm told on a regular basis that his body was repatriated to the United States. "Oh, really? Where?" These people are resolute in their belief, if short on the details. They'll keep insisting until I tell them Jim is still buried six feet under in a corner of Division 6. Nobody repatriated his remains. I checked the registers, and there's no trace of exhumation in the singer's sizable file; the story's pure fiction. Nonetheless, news outlets and social media platforms continue to spread the rumor. I had to vigorously refute the claims to a journalist who was writing a story about Morrison in honor of the fiftieth anniversary of his death.

◇◇◇◇◇

TODAY, PEOPLE RARELY leave joints and bottles of whiskey on Jim Morrison's grave. Instead, the fans who manage to jump the fence leave a hodgepodge of kitschy curios and trinkets—cherubs, multicolored windmills, plastic flowers, bird figurines, framed pictures, drawings, love letters, and sheet music. Then there are the unconventional offerings, like wine bottles, lighters, rolling paper, and incense sticks. Everyone honors the rock star's memory in their own way. Incidentally, the fans I've spoken to were all very gracious, compassionate, and... sober. Managing Jim Morrison's grave comes with unique challenges, but it's no longer a cause of major concern.

About a decade ago, a new ritual began to emerge: sightseers started sticking their chewing gum to the tree closest to the grave. It's a childish way of letting the world know you visited the mythical site. An act of rebellion worthy of the singer himself, albeit a far cry from the excesses of the early years. It's almost beautiful in its ugliness, though quite unsanitary. When several new wads appear, the air starts to reek of rancid strawberries or stale mint. Some people get creative and mold their gum into various shapes, while others use theirs to hold cigarette butts, metro tickets, or guitar picks. The tree is covered in little notes and drawings, a testament to the cult following Morrison continues to attract a half century after his death. As with all rituals that develop in Père-Lachaise, nobody knows who started it. People jumped on the bandwagon, and the chewing-gum tree was born. The tree seems to be taking everything in stride, even if it had to be wrapped in bamboo fencing to shield it from the "tributes" to its famous neighbor. It will forever wear this protective covering like a shoe—the tree equivalent of stepping in gum.

No Dead-End Jobs Here

WORKING IN DEATH CARE isn't glamorous. It's a little-known, unattractive sector (as evidenced by my hiring process) that few people are familiar with. It's rarely a calling and more often the result of happenstance. But once you have your foot in the door, the industry's unexpected riches make it very difficult to leave. What begins as a job turns into a vocation.

The funeral industry employs a wide variety of professionals, most of whom are passionate about their work and wouldn't dream of changing careers. I know a number of people who had to leave the business but who still feel nostalgic for their days on the job. While it's very difficult to recruit staff, those who give the sector a try generally stay until they retire. A career in death care may seem unappealing, to put it lightly, but these jobs can be fascinating.

Working in a cemetery isn't just about digging graves or raising a gate to let the hearse through. A range of tasks are carried out by a multitude of professionals, all working together to perform one of the most beautiful public services there is.

◇◇◇◇◇

I STRUGGLE TO DEFINE my job since my exact role is so multifaceted. In reality, I devote most of my time to the following three duties: coordinating the work of the

Dedicated to preserving memory

While the concession system helped to preserve the individual memories of ordinary families and public figures, Père-Lachaise also plays a crucial role in preserving collective memory. The cemetery's best-known memorial is unquestionably the Communards' Wall, where thousands of people gather each May to honor the memory of the Paris Commune. A memorial to commemorate Holocaust victims whose bodies were never recovered includes fifteen deeply moving monuments, one for each concentration camp. Père-Lachaise also bears witness to history with memorials to honor fallen soldiers and victims of the wars France has fought: the Franco-Prussian War, World War I, World War II, and the Algerian War. Monuments across the cemetery honor the victims of major fires (Bazar de la Charité in 1897, eighty-member team I lead (administrative staff, security guards, groundskeepers, and gravediggers); managing state-regulated land (issuing and repossessing funeral concessions); and responding to user requests.

It's impossible to describe a typical workday with all its hustle and bustle. On any given day I'll sign paperwork, answer emails and paper correspondence, meet with a family about a plot sale, touch base with support staff, manage schedules, untangle a legal issue regarding a funeral procession, supervise a sensitive exhumation, complete a reporting

---

Opéra-Comique in 1887), aircraft accidents (Turkish Airlines Flight 981, West Caribbean Airways Flight 708, Flash Airlines Flight 604, Air France Flight 477), and more. It's impossible to include an exhaustive list of memorials here, but they are what makes Père-Lachaise a uniquely diverse commemorative site. Each year, around 150 ceremonies are organized by various groups and held in front of these monuments or celebrity graves. The number of participants can range from just a few to several thousand, which means security arrangements must be adapted each time. On Saturday, May 29, 2021, Les Amies et Amis de la Commune de Paris 1871 set the record by gathering twelve thousand people to celebrate the 150th anniversary of the uprising.

table, design a poster, remind visitors of cemetery rules, sign more paperwork, answer more emails, scout locations with a movie director for an upcoming shoot, review security arrangements in preparation for a celebrity burial, compile a list of abandoned plots to repossess, get on a conference call to discuss budgetary decisions, manage staff, lead a team meeting, respond to management requests, hire a plumber to deal with a leak, call a computer technician about an IT problem, meet with a disgruntled visitor, secure a dangerous burial plot, write up a report, send information up or down the ladder, authorize a commemorative ceremony, sign more paperwork, answer more emails, and so on.

Because my job is so diverse, I've developed a wide range of skills and knowledge in different fields: funeral law, human resources, workplace health and safety, grief counseling, funeral rites, and more. It's a demanding, time-consuming job unlike any other. It requires a great deal of versatility, but it's enormously rewarding. It involves being overwhelmed on a regular basis and knowing that's totally normal. It's feeling like you're a Swiss army knife because your various skills are constantly being solicited. Not knowing what my day will look like when I walk into my office every morning is actually my favorite part of the job.

◇◇◇◇

DESPITE MY MANY duties, it would be arrogant to claim that I carry the entire cemetery on my shoulders. Dozens of people come to work in Père-Lachaise every day. I rely on a team of colleagues led by Jérôme, my indispensable associate curator. Without him, I'd have worked myself to death a long time ago. We work closely to oversee not only Père-Lachaise but also its four satellite cemeteries: Belleville, Bercy, Charonne, and La Villette.

A cemetery can't exist without buildings, perimeter walls, vehicles, staff rooms, offices, supplies, and more. These material aspects are managed by Philippe, my operations coordinator, who does a remarkable job behind the scenes to make sure every part of the machine runs smoothly.

Finally, there are all the other professionals and middle managers without whom Père-Lachaise wouldn't be able to function 365 days a year. The picture wouldn't be complete if I didn't mention the host of other professionals who keep Père-Lachaise buzzing with activity from the moment the gates open.

◇◇◇◇◇

SO, WHO WORKS in Père-Lachaise? I've compiled a list of job descriptions to introduce readers to our professions—and, while I'm at it, possibly drum up some interest in the industry.

Security Guards

Thirty-two agents are hired to guard the entrances, carry out security patrols, welcome visitors, and answer questions. They oversee all funeral operations (burials, ash scatterings, exhumations) and write reports, which are archived in the cemetery records. They help tourists locate celebrity graves, turn away joggers, and remind anyone who may have forgotten that Père-Lachaise is first and foremost a cemetery where good manners, respect, and tranquility are essential.

Administrative Staff

The cemetery's nine administrative staff members manage the 96,600 burial concessions, process the 3,500 operations carried out each year, and handle the archives. The job requires a broad skill set combined with rigor and resourcefulness. Fully versed in funeral law, administrative staff can answer any question families might have about their concessions. They provide information about durations and price, renewals and conversions, the number of spaces available, who is buried, possible exhumations, remains transfers, and more.

Arborists

Père-Lachaise's tree heritage is just as important as its funerary heritage. While the intertwining of vegetable and mineral has become a trademark of the cemetery, it makes life difficult for the municipal arborists tasked with caring for its four thousand trees (pruning, felling, and planting). It can be challenging to access the trees given the graves and rocky terrain, but it's important to keep them healthy: a fallen branch could cause irreparable damage. Yet any time arborists take down a sick tree, they're labeled "criminals" by the self-proclaimed forestry experts who've read *The Hidden Life of Trees*. Arborists do, however, have one undisputed privilege: they get to admire Père-Lachaise from the treetops.

Concessions Officers

If you're looking to transfer the remains of an ancestor to an ossuary in order to make room in the family vault for new bodies, or if you want to know how to pass on a concession to a nephew, contact a concessions officer. Located in a building in Division 83, these professionals can answer any legal question a concession holder might have. Their department is responsible for ensuring that exhumation requests in each of Paris's twenty cemeteries are submitted by the deceased's next of kin, in accordance with the law. Concessions officers also oversee the extremely complex matter of concession transfers. Like property lawyers for the funeral industry, concessions officers must verify the legal status of supposed heirs before they can be recognized as the rightful beneficiaries.

Groundskeepers

With their yellow vests and noisy leaf blowers, Père-Lachaise's twenty groundskeepers are hard to miss. They rake leaves, remove garbage, sweep paths, and keep the cemetery clean. Since pesticides were banned in 2015, groundskeepers are also responsible for weeding the cemetery's cobbled avenues and sidewalks to clear the way for foot traffic. Between the leaves that fall in autumn and the grass that grows in spring, their job never ends. A Sisyphean task at Père-Lachaise.

Heritage Conservationists

Parisian cemeteries boast a considerable funerary heritage, but, like the memory of the deceased, it is crumbling. Heritage

conservationists, led by a heritage curator, are responsible for inventorying, restoring, and promoting Père-Lachaise's exceptional cultural patrimony. Each burial plot that has been abandoned and repossessed is thoroughly examined to determine whether it can be destroyed or should be preserved for its heritage or historical value. An indispensable job.

Crematorium Employees

Opened in 1889, France's first crematorium is now run by a private company as part of a public service delegation agreement. The neo-Byzantine structure, designed by Jean Camille Formigé, is one of the cemetery's most important buildings. With the rise in cremation, celebrants and operators carry out almost six thousand cremations a year. The prestigious Salle de la Coupole in the crematorium building is regularly used for celebrity funerals.

Construction Workers

Uneven cobblestones, rusted handrails, broken stairs... Père-Lachaise is no spring chicken! Each year, the Division of Cemeteries' Public Works department allocates a large part of its budget to restoring paths, walls, and buildings that date back to 1804. Construction teams are on site throughout the year to perform ongoing work that ensures visitor safety and preserves the life of the cemetery.

Florists

Wreaths, casket sprays, bouquets, hearts, and more: each day, florists deliver flower arrangements to the crematorium and grave sites. Flowers are one of the most popular ways to pay respect to the deceased and offer condolences to the family, often with a sympathy card attached. Each flower has a different meaning associated with its shape and color. Florists design their arrangements to reflect the age and personality of the deceased as well as the flower-giver's relationship with them.

Gravediggers

Though gravediggers definitely have an image problem, it would be impossible to run a cemetery without them. All in top physical shape, Père-Lachaise's eight gravediggers are responsible for demolishing abandoned graves that the City has repossessed, exhuming remains, and transferring them to the ossuary. They make it possible for new plots to be issued to families across Paris. And while they spend a great deal of time underground handling bones, they certainly aren't in low spirits. They take great pride in what they do and would tell you it's a job like any other—even though that's clearly not true.

Site Supervisors

Each year, around 1,600 work orders are performed on graves across the cemetery. These include general maintenance, vault repair, gravestone conservation, monument installation, chapel restoration, painting, engraving, attaching a headstone photo, and more. Site supervisors oversee the quality of the work, coordinate with a Buildings of France architect to install new monuments (or with the regional Conservation of Historical Monuments office in the case of a restoration), and ensure all monuments conform to Paris cemetery regulations.

Headstone Engravers

Often, we can locate these professionals from a distance due to the faint "tap-tap-tapping" they make each time their chisel comes into contact with the headstone, etching for all eternity the names of the cemetery's newest residents. Their work marks the end of the funeral process, as if inscribing the name of the deceased gives a finality to their death. It's a solitary profession carried out within the calm of the cemetery. Sun shades and portable radios are indispensable tools of the job. On occasion, headstone engravers must contort their bodies into uncomfortable, almost comical positions to carry out a family's wishes. Their greatest fear is making a mistake: imagine spelling a name incorrectly or putting it on the wrong tomb.

Gardeners

Père-Lachaise was originally designed as an ornamental garden. While its green spaces have shrunk considerably after two centuries of use, its flora is preserved thanks to the five gardeners who plant, trim, and maintain the flower beds and shrubbery within the divisions and at some of the cemetery's most iconic sites (such as the East Chapel, crematorium, and Communards' Wall). The gardeners' busiest period is undoubtedly in the run-up to All Saints' Day when, much to the delight of families, they plant thousands of brightly colored chrysanthemums.

Monument Makers

These professionals work behind the scenes, outside, and occasionally in harsh weather conditions to perform a service that's poorly recognized and underappreciated. The layout of Père-Lachaise makes their job very demanding, since, unlike in modern cemeteries, access to burial plots is often limited. Building a vault into sloped terrain or installing a monument weighing several tons in the middle of a division with no vehicle access requires great skill, attention to detail, and strategy—along with excellent physical fitness. Monument makers also perform exhumations at the request of families, which can be a heart-wrenching task. Theirs is a thankless profession often performed in the shadows.

Funeral Parlor Employees

Funeral consultants, celebrants, pallbearers, funeral attendants—these professions tend to be unpopular. Yet sooner or later, everyone will need to call the undertaker, a job in constant evolution. As the influence of religion declines, celebrants are being asked to play a more central role in personalized and non-faith-based ceremonies. The sector itself is far from in decline, however; according to data reported by the French National Institute of Statistics, deaths will continue to rise until 2050 as the baby boomers (people born between 1945 and 1964) age. Looking to change careers? The funeral industry has some promising leads...

Religious Leaders

Although French cemeteries have been officially secular spaces since 1881, a law from around the same time guarantees individuals the right to a funeral ceremony of their religion of choice. Every day, leaders of different faiths officiate funerals at the cemetery, either in a multifaith chapel in the crematorium, at the graveside, or, for Catholic ceremonies, in the East Chapel. From priests to rabbis, imams, pastors, deacons, and more, the religious leaders who walk the cemetery's paths are as diverse as the communities that coexist in Paris.

Division of Cemeteries Staff

Located in Division 83, where it's nestled beneath a canopy of trees, the Division of Cemeteries coordinates the operations of all twenty Parisian cemeteries. Employees provide technical, budgetary, logistical, legal, administrative, and general assistance on a daily basis, making it a vital support system.

VIP Treatment

Père-Lachaise is the most-visited cemetery in the world thanks to the large number of celebrities who, like Jim Morrison, have made it their final resting place. These figures have marked eras, influenced styles, and shaped fashions. In short, they've changed our lives. Their contributions are still being studied, performed, and commemorated. Street signs and public squares bear their names. Together, they are what makes Père-Lachaise an open-air Pantheon.

Interred within its walls are some of the biggest names in literature (Wilde, Balzac, Proust, Colette, Apollinaire, Musset, Molière, La Fontaine, Beaumarchais, Stein and Toklas, Richard Wright), music (Morrison, Piaf, Chopin, Bellini, Callas, Poulenc, Cherubini, Bizet, Bashung, Michel Legrand, Michel Petrucciani), cinema (Méliès, Chabrol, Ophüls, Annie Girardot, Yves Montand and Simone Signoret, Gaspard

Ulliel), theater (Sarah Bernhardt, Marcel Marceau, Mademoiselle Mars), painting (Modigliani, Caillebotte, Pissarro, David, Delacroix, Géricault, Ingres, Seurat, Ernst), architecture (Brongniart, Visconti), sculpture (Bartholomé, Falguière, Clésinger, David d'Angers, Arman), gastronomy (Parmentier, Brillat-Savarin, Menier, Ladurée), dance (Isadora Duncan, Serge Peretti, Jane Avril), science and technology (Monge, Champollion, Fourier, Claude Bernard, Gay-Lussac, Breguet, Cuvier, Bienvenüe), and political and military leaders (Sieyès, Faure, Haussmann, Thiers, Kellermann, André Masséna, Michel Ney), to name but a few.

This list is by no means exhaustive; one attempt to inventory Père-Lachaise's notable figures put the count at nearly

Lights, camera, action!

Père-Lachaise hosts a large number of movie and TV productions. From arthouse cinema to Bollywood, Netflix, and Disney+, directors from all over the world come to shoot scenes—unsurprisingly, mostly funerals. The site's romanticism also lends itself well to meet-cutes featuring either brilliant or terribly clichéd dialogue—there's hardly anything in between. A few film scenes are particularly memorable: the segment directed by Wes Craven in *Paris, je t'aime* that features a couple on the verge of breaking up as they wander around the cemetery before reconciling in front of Oscar Wilde's grave; the one where actor Denis Lavant is wholly

4,500. While this includes the superstars everybody knows, the vast majority of names are of lesser renown. Yet, at one time or another, these individuals left their mark on their respective fields. They were the influencers of their era—not in today's overused sense of the term, but to the extent that decades after their death, their reputations are known to historians, associations, and tombstone tourists. In fact, new names are constantly being added to the register thanks to queries we receive from the public. Quite recently, for example, we were able to record the graves of Boris Bazhanov (Stalin's personal secretary), Edmond Audemars (cyclist and aviator), Shi Pei Pu (Chinese opera singer and spy), and Marie-Jean Desouches (credited with inventing the folding

possessed in Leos Carax's *Holy Motors*. On television, Père-Lachaise has recently featured in *Emily in Paris* and *Lupin*.

Filming at Père-Lachaise requires a great deal of preparation. We coordinate with the director and technical teams to balance the quality of the shot with the decorum the site demands. Production teams are always given access to a dummy grave to simulate a burial. But out of respect for the dead, chase scenes or those featuring a gunfight in the cemetery are strictly prohibited. James Bond is unlikely to make an appearance at Père-Lachaise anytime soon.

bed used by Napoleon and his generals during military campaigns).

I devote part of my time to learning the stories of these individuals and the larger historical context surrounding them. I find this aspect of my job very enriching, and it gives me a break from the daily grind of the funerary machine. While doing paperwork, in fact, I've occasionally come across an individual who played a decisive role in history. This was the case for Malvina Poulain. Her file didn't mention any political activity, but one detail caught my attention: among a list of names, hers was circled in red. Why the color code? I was intrigued. A quick internet search revealed that Malvina Poulain had been a Communard with ties to Louise Michel, one of the major figures of the Paris Commune. As far as my predecessors were concerned, she was probably a "red." Thanks to this lucky find, we can now say a female revolutionary is buried in Père-Lachaise. (Until that point, only male Communards had been recorded.)

When people think of Père-Lachaise, they often associate it with great men and tend to overlook the illustrious women buried there. In recent years, a number of initiatives, including guided tours and books like Camille Paix's *Mère Lachaise*, have begun calling attention to the cemetery's great women. And there are so many! From artists (photographer Gerda Taro and painter Rosa Bonheur) to feminist activists (journalist Hubertine Auclert, writer Monique Wittig, and lawyer Gisèle Halimi), scores of residents fought for women's liberation or used their talents to revolutionize the art world.

UNFORTUNATELY, SOME CELEBRITIES no longer have families to tend to their graves and, as a result, their appearance suffers. When this happens, visitors often misinterpret the untidy plots as a sign of a citywide failure to perform necessary upkeep or maintenance duties. It's important to remember that the graves in Père-Lachaise—famous or not—are private property over which the administration has no authority. The only solution, where legally possible, is to open a repossession claim on the grounds of abandonment. Once a grave that has been ravaged by time becomes the property of the municipal government, the City of Paris will incur the restoration costs. The graves of writers Élisa Mercoeur and Honoré de Balzac have both benefited from this procedure.

Caring for the final resting places of such legends is both a responsibility and an honor. Their presence in the cemetery, along with the queries I field from curious visitors, makes me want to learn more about these individuals' careers, their bodies of work, and their lives—their successes and failures, their romantic pursuits, and their final hours. It becomes an almost personal relationship; I end up feeling like I know them, yet I remain humbled by their genius. Because of what they represent and their unique relationship with the public, their graves are the object of special attention. Whenever there's a storm, the first grave I check on is Chopin's, because it sits a stone's throw from several trees. When singer Ahmet Kaya's grave was vandalized on November 13, 2021, it sparked outrage in the Kurdish community. We made every effort to support his family and loved ones throughout the traumatic ordeal.

YESTERDAY'S STARS HAVE FADED, and today's stars will follow suit. Celebrity is ever-changing. The legacy of poet Jacques Delille, buried to much fanfare in 1813, has been lost to time. The tombs of Marshal Ney or of law student Nicolas Lallemand, killed by a royal guard during a June 1820 student protest, were once pilgrimage sites that were covered in graffiti long before Jim Morrison's. Similarly, Oscar Wilde's grave was covered in lipstick kisses left by adoring fans until it was restored in 2011. The ritual damaged the stone, now a designated historical monument and prompted Wilde's descendants to install a plexiglass barrier around it. His grave is still among the most visited at Père-Lachaise, but the lipstick stains have since migrated to singer Alain Bashung's headstone.

Will Jim Morrison eventually be dethroned in terms of popularity? Johnny Hallyday certainly came close. The "French Elvis" was supposed to be buried in Père-Lachaise, but family members decided otherwise. When I picture what that would have meant, it gives me chills: a never-ending parade of admirers, the incessant clack of cowboy boots against the cobblestones, the hit songs echoing down the paths, the thousands of fans that would show up each year on his birthday, the difficult closing times and nightly intrusions by people desperate to spend a night alongside their idol, the inevitable rock 'n' roll graffiti and talismans left on his grave, and more. All in all, I'm glad he's buried in St. Bart's, in the Caribbean. It's selfish, I admit—but it's saved me a lot of worry.

OTHER GIANTS ARE conspicuously absent. Victor Hugo should have been buried in his family plot, which is located in Division 26. Instead, his proud homeland declared a state funeral for its native son, and on June 1, 1885, the man who "became immortal in life" was escorted to the Pantheon by nearly two million people.

According to historians, Napoleon, the "father" of Père-Lachaise, wanted to be laid to rest beside "his" marshals. But, forced into exile, he was buried on the island of Saint Helena. Later, his remains were transferred to Les Invalides.

Some luminaries made a stop in Père-Lachaise but no longer reside here today. Such is the case for Maria Callas, whose ashes were placed in the columbarium before being scattered over the Aegean Sea. Similarly, the remains of resistance leader Jean Moulin and activist Victor Schœlcher were transferred to the Pantheon. The administration decided not to reallocate the columbarium niches where Callas and Moulin rested for a time; today, a plaque honors their memory. Schœlcher's tomb, and its high-relief sculpture by Alexis-Hippolyte Fromanger, still stands along the Avenue de Saint-Morys as a shrine to the abolitionist.

Finally, there are the public figures who journalists claim are being "buried in Père-Lachaise," while in reality it's just their memorial service that's being held in the crematorium's dome hall. This type of information, reposted again and again on social media, often confuses fans, and it falls to us to set the record straight. Most recently, this was the case for the actor Jean-Paul Belmondo and the singer Régine.

CELEBRITY OFTEN GOES hand-in-hand with scandal (actress Béatrice Dalle sparked a social media frenzy when she was pictured rolling a joint on singer Mano Solo's grave), outsized demands (writer and chess enthusiast Raymond Roussel is interred alone in a vault containing thirty-two compartments, or half the number of squares on a chess board), and the whims of stardom. Such is the case with Alfred de Musset, whose epitaph spells out his last wishes:

> My dear friends, when I die,
> Plant a willow in the cemetery.
> Leaves that weep under the sky;
> Its pallor is sweet and dear to me,
> And in the shade of the tree
> Beneath the earth I shall lie.

We take Musset's willow seriously. But try as we might to fulfill his dying wish, our good intentions always fall short. For decades, despite sustained efforts to respect Musset's words from beyond the grave, the willows planted and replanted continue to die prematurely. The nature of the soil isn't a good match for this species of tree, which does best in moist, cool earth. The most recent willow, planted in 2020, is a variety that can supposedly adapt to dry soil. We wish it a long life.

⋄⋄⋄⋄⋄

WHENEVER A CELEBRITY dies, I don't need to read the notifications that flood my phone. I usually find out first from family or friends, whose text messages have a familiar refrain: "Will it be Père-Lachaise?" My colleagues or superiors ask more or less the same thing: "Are you getting this one?" Often, the answer is no. Not everyone is buried in Père-Lachaise; far from it! Let's be honest, the cemetery is no longer "the place to be forever." Père-Lachaise faces stiff competition from Montmartre and Montparnasse, which became trendier in Left Bank circles after Jean-Paul Sartre was buried there in the early 1980s. Like Serge Gainsbourg, Mireille Darc, and Jacques Chirac, the cultural and political elites now lean toward the more centrally located charms of nearby Saint-Germain-des-Prés. Père-Lachaise is in a working-class neighborhood, and despite its flashy reputation, it's for ordinary Parisians. That's just as well, really. So far in my tenure, eleven thousand people have been buried or had their ashes scattered in Père-Lachaise. Only a handful of these have been celebrities, including Joseph Joffo, Michel Legrand, Marie Laforêt, Anna Karina, Manu Dibango, Idir, Gisèle Halimi, Claude Brasseur, Ivry Gitlis, Étienne Mougeotte, Gaspard Ulliel, and Thierry Mugler.

Each time a public figure dies, it sends ripples through the small world of the Paris funeral industry. Where will they be laid to rest? Which funeral parlor will provide the service? Will they be buried or cremated? We all ask the same questions; we all scour the internet for interviews or clips in which the star may have expressed their last wishes. We don't have an unhealthy obsession; we're just doing our professional duty!

Although celebrity funerals are rare, they always have a major impact on the cemetery's operations. Take composer

Michel Legrand's 2019 funeral, which attracted a great deal of media coverage. On January 27, journalists began reporting that the service would take place in Père-Lachaise on February 1, but I was unaware of this development. His wife, Macha Méril, had arranged a meeting with me to purchase a plot, but I didn't realize the funeral date had been set. Sometimes I have to read the news to know what's going on in my own cemetery.

Whenever a high-profile funeral in Père-Lachaise is announced to great fanfare, the next day our phones begin ringing off the hook. Suddenly, it seems that everyone wants to purchase a plot here for their final resting place. If Michel Legrand was able to secure a plot, that must mean space is available. Would there happen to be one for them? We tell these people what we tell everyone: a plot in Père-Lachaise can only be granted at the time of death and under certain conditions.

During a January 30 radio interview, Méril announced that she'd secured a plot for Legrand in Père-Lachaise and knew he'd be happy to learn his resting place wasn't far from Francis Lemarque, a good friend and fellow composer who'd collaborated with him on *The Umbrellas of Cherbourg*. It was nonetheless a coincidence that the friends ended up near each other. When it comes to public figures, like my predecessors, I try to avoid making the same mistake as with Jim Morrison; whenever possible, I find plots that are accessible and not as hemmed in. The goal is to make it easy to find them and maintain order for families whose plots are nearby. Hordes of tourists aren't conducive to paying your respects to the dead. It's also for safety reasons on the day of the funeral, since VIP burials frequently attract large crowds including cultural icons, government leaders, elected officials, fans, curious bystanders, and journalists. We coordinate with national and municipal authorities to implement measures that will ensure the safety and happiness of the family. For Legrand's funeral, barricades and a greater police presence afforded the family relative privacy.

Some families want burials to be strictly private affairs. For this to happen, the press mustn't be informed of the location, date, or time. Even then, we implement a few security measures—this was the case for Marie Laforêt—just in case there are any media leaks.

Whether they're publicized or not, high-profile funerals are exceptional events that add a welcome splash of glamour to my job. But as with most other deaths, the people left behind (partner, children, friends, manager, or press agent) are frequently too overwhelmed to organize the funeral. My role is to support them as best I can so they can do what matters most: give their loved one a send-off worthy of their career, before the curtain falls for the last time.

The Same World

I KNOW A NUMBER of Parisians who tell me they want to leave the city, citing a need to reconnect with nature, hear the birds sing, or breathe in the smell of freshly cut grass. The pandemic lockdowns spurred many of them to take the plunge. While I can understand where they're coming from, I have no desire to follow suit. I grew up in the countryside, in a village of about two thousand people. As a teen, my greatest luxury was to take the train to "the city" once a month and spend my allowance at book and multimedia chains Fnac or Gibert Joseph.

Living in Paris is like a dream come true. Why would I move back to the countryside? I love Paris because I can do things that would be impossible in more rural areas, like go food shopping between noon and two PM or admire the deserted quays of the Seine on an early morning run. Oddly enough, these days I never go to Gibert Joseph and only rarely to Fnac.

Still, I regularly feel the need to reconnect with nature, as all Parisians do. For this, I have an easy fix: Père-Lachaise itself can make me feel like I'm living in the countryside. In the middle of Paris, the cemetery offers me the chance to hear silence, to see a range of wildflowers, and to observe a wide variety of animals. I may have grown up in a village surrounded by fields, but I see more wild animals now that I live and work in Père-Lachaise, the largest green space within Paris city limits.

⋄⋄⋄⋄⋄

WHILE PÈRE-LACHAISE'S ECOLOGICAL BENEFITS are now clear, its role in promoting biodiversity is actually quite recent. After decades during which the administration waged outright war on plant life, the vegetation is finally coming back with a vengeance.

While Père-Lachaise was abundantly green in its early years—remember, Brongniart had designed the cemetery as an English-style garden—the flora was scaled down drastically over the course of the nineteenth century. A victim of its own success, the cemetery was forced to cut back its foliage over time to make room for new plots that would meet the growing demand for perpetual concessions. Subdividing wasn't enough, though, and Père-Lachaise was expanded five times over the years. The largest and final extension in 1850 added forty-two acres to the site. The flat terrain of this section, located on what was the Charonne plateau, contrasted sharply with the rugged features of the original cemetery, which had been built into the hillside of the former Jesuit property. In what would become Divisions 80 to 97, graves were perfectly aligned in a grid pattern that left almost no room for vegetation; greenery was an afterthought. Nothing but the trees that were planted along the paths and a few boxy hedges timidly distinguished one section from another.

Paradoxically, the funeral monuments that began to emerge were often, at the request of their owners, covered with flowers! Floral motifs weren't solely ornamental; each flower or plant was meant to convey a specific meaning. Pansies symbolize memory, poppies are associated with eternal sleep, everlasting flowers—like their name suggests—are synonymous with immortality, ivy is a symbol of devotion, lilies represent purity, laurel stands for eternal glory, thistles indicate suffering, palm leaves represent victory or achievement, and the list goes on. These floral motifs can be found on tombstones and on chapel doors and facades, most often in bas-relief.

Over the course of the twentieth century, pesticides were introduced, swiftly killing off the last of the cemetery's wildflowers. Artificial flowers hit the market at just the right time, and their many advantages quickly won over families: the plastic blooms were affordable, didn't need to be watered, and could last several years.

◇◇◇◇◇

AS THE EXPRESSION GOES, self-preservation is the first law of nature. Père-Lachaise was no exception. The first to revolt were the trees, which defied their orderly rows almost immediately to extend their grip on the stone monuments.

Whether the product of a windblown seed or a sucker from a nearby tree, they all have one thing in common: they grew in an unruly snarl over graves that had been abandoned. In some areas, the evidence of nature taking back its rights is a spectacle to behold. Roots spread out like tentacles and coil around graves, tree trunks split the headstones they have partially or wholly consumed, and metal rods, the vestiges of old railings, can be seen poking up through the trees that have devoured them.

The most brazen didn't hesitate to attack even the chapels. Here, the roots of a maple have burst through the joints of one monument. There, a black locust has sprouted up through another and pierced its cupola. Nearby, a plane tree has embedded itself in the soil of a long-overgrown chapel roof. Père-Lachaise aficionados like to say these gravestone-eating trees are "necrophagous." Most can be found in the romantic sector of the cemetery, so named for the convergence of life and death.

Today, the four thousand trees that call the cemetery home represent more than eighty different species—or roughly one tree for every seventeen graves. The most common types are chestnuts, maples, ashes, oaks, planes, thujas, and lindens. Père-Lachaise also boasts nine standout specimens, including the magnificent horse chestnut located beside the Communards' Wall. Planted in 1880, the remarkable tree now rises sixty-five feet in the air, with a trunk measuring eleven feet in circumference. It's well worth a detour. Walk through Division 75 and you'll see a gutta-percha, a "gum tree" native to Asia that gets its nickname from the stringy, rubberlike sap it produces. Finally, many shrubs have taken up residence in the abandoned planters scattered throughout the cemetery. What they lack in size, they make up for in value by helping to maintain the area's biodiversity.

◇◇◇◇◇

IN ADDITION TO Père-Lachaise's rich tree heritage, the cemetery now features a wealth of greenery that staged a comeback after pesticides were banned in 2015. Sidewalks, pathways, and abandoned planters sprouted wildflowers that multiplied, unbidden, between graves and in every last corner of the cemetery. The walkways are flush with a variety of species, including wood avens, dandelions, garlic mustard, woodland forget-me-nots, greater celandine, lawn daisies, and yellow toadflax. Wild orchids like the broad-leaved helleborine are also making a dazzling return. Groundskeepers make every effort to avoid mowing over flowering plants such as columbines, daisies, marigolds, and grape hyacinths. With their distinct shapes and bright colors, they make the cemetery more beautiful.

Roberts geraniums or Kenilworth ivy slip easily through cracks in the stone graves, while climbing ivy simply grows over them. Different types of ferns splay their ruffled foliage across walls throughout the grounds. Nature certainly has a sense of irony: over the last few years, several species of wildflowers have taken root in the cemetery's arid plateau, where nature had been practically stamped out following the 1850 expansion. The shiny geranium, which doesn't typically grow in the greater Paris region, has been spotted in

Division 92. Each spring in Division 81, visitors can admire the smallflower buttercup (*Ranunculus parviflorus*), classified in France as an endangered species.

Sometimes, when conditions make it impossible for wildflowers to grow on their own, we'll give them a little help. Within the divisions, gravediggers have been gradually removing the paving slabs that decades ago families were allowed to lay at the foot of their graves, and replacing them with soil that will re-nature over time. Gardeners are covering the sidewalks with rolls of sod grown in the city's greenhouses or planting lawn seed composed mainly of clover. So far, 88,000 square feet of sidewalks have been

Small potatoes

Antoine-Augustin Parmentier, an army pharmacist and agronomist, was a lifelong advocate of the potato as a food source. He discovered the tuber's value in Prussia, where he was imprisoned during the Seven Years' War (1756–63).

In France, the potato wasn't officially declared edible until 1772, and even then, the French would spend years arguing that potatoes were only suitable for pig feed. But Parmentier was undeterred. He continued his efforts to popularize the potato until Louis XVI allowed him to plant fifty-four acres of the crop. The king's authorization changed the image of the spud in France; with a place at the royal table, it was no longer a food for the poor. The potato became a staple of grassed over since 2016—and that's just the beginning! The goal is an entirely rewilded Père-Lachaise.

⬦⬦⬦⬦⬦

I DON'T BELIEVE there is historical data to document the evolution of the cemetery's animal life, but Père-Lachaise was likely home to foxes before they had to compete for space with the dead and before the surrounding area urbanized. Birds, on the other hand, have always been abundant thanks to the cemetery's many trees.

Like plants, animals are frequently depicted on gravestones according to their own particular symbolism. Dogs,

---

French cuisine, taking many different forms and served with a variety of sauces.

As a tribute to Parmentier, enthusiasts of the french fry and shepherd's pie (called *hachis Parmentier* in French) leave potatoes on his grave, sometimes with a touch of originality. Recently, for instance, I came across a very chic potato sporting a bow tie.

The delicate bas-reliefs that decorate Parmentier's tomb in Division 39 include depictions of a farming tool and the plants he studied. Today, his resting place is to Père-Lachaise what the potato is to our diet: an absolute staple.

of course, are a symbol of loyalty. Butterflies, owing to their short life span, underscore the ephemeral nature of life. Because they can see at night, owls represent wisdom, or victory over darkness. Snakes are a symbol of healing or regeneration; doctors' tombstones often feature a snake wrapped around the rod of Asclepius. The image of a pelican feeding its young from its own blood is a symbol of sacrifice and parental love. Bees represent hard work, and doves stand for innocence.

Some animals—living ones, not carved—also have a close relationship to the graves. Cats like basking on the headstones, using them as beds or for shelter in inclement weather. They don't play favorites and can adapt to anything: limestone chapels, marble caskets, granite tombs, even planters. Evidently, their purring doesn't disturb the eternal sleep of the dead as they nap alongside them, sometimes for hours. The cats have become such constant companions in the cemetery that they almost seem to melt into the commemorative art itself, to the delight of visitors who regularly fall under their spell. But there aren't enough cats to go around, and not every resident gets to enjoy a warm belly. There are no waiting lists, and the cats choose their stone beds on a whim. This fusion of animal and mineral often seems so complete that I've started calling them "tombcats."

Other, lesser-known animals round out Père-Lachaise's astonishing menagerie. The stone marten, a small nocturnal creature about twenty inches long, sleeps in abandoned vaults by day and searches for food by night. (See pages 36 and 193.) Stone martens have a reputation for killing chickens and producing an awful stench, but I have a soft spot for them. I love to watch them toddle around, bobbing their hindquarters as they go. They're remarkably agile animals that can slip between tombs and scale trees and chapel roofs in record time. I rarely come across stone martens, but whenever I do, they manage to both thrill and baffle me. I've lost count of the number of times my enthusiasm has caused me to miss a shot. I've also learned that there's no point seeking them out. A sighting is a mystery to which only they hold the key—and it's precisely this unpredictability that makes them so precious. When fortune smiles on me, stone martens can be quite curious, pulling themselves onto a monument and posing for the camera. These encounters always last long enough for me to wonder what the animal is thinking. "Him again?" "Go back to your foxes!" "Do you expect me to smile?" Although we have nothing in common, our eyes meet and we acknowledge each other. And despite our differences, we realize that we're a part of the same world.

◇◇◇◇◇

THE RESURGENCE OF wild plants and animals at Père-Lachaise raises the question: What is their place in this ecosystem? In a space designed for and by humans, is it possible to embrace flora and fauna? We tried—and failed—to eradicate the nature around us, only to reproduce it extensively on the monuments we erect. A few of the cemetery walkways have even been named in nature's honor: Chemin du Coq ("Rooster Way"), Chemin des Chèvres ("Goat Way") or Avenue des Acacias.

Not everyone is thrilled by the vegetation springing up between the graves. Some people seem nostalgic for a Père-Lachaise free of the "weeds" they associate with poor maintenance and a lack of respect for the dead. Incredibly, I once received a letter from a Mrs. Lapoussière (in French, "Dust") complaining that the cemetery had become too dirty. On the whole, however, we receive fewer complaints with each passing year as nature reclaims its rights and biodiversity triumphs. In 2018, beehives were installed in Division 78; in 2022, fifteen grape plants were planted along the walls of Divisions 75 and 76; a dozen birdhouses are slated to be hung from trees to encourage nesting. Together, these initiatives are meant to promote life within Père-Lachaise and, more broadly, to expand the role of both flora and fauna in our increasingly urbanized societies. Since we have such a palpable need to reconnect with nature—especially those of us living in metropolitan areas—and since nature is so vital to our well-being, why shouldn't cemeteries do their part?

◇◇◇◇◇

IT'S IMPORTANT TO KNOW how to observe nature, how to truly see it. I was a complete novice. I never imagined I'd see such rich biodiversity in the heart of Paris, never guessed that almost every night I'd have a chance to watch, enthralled, as the lives of a family of foxes unfolded within the city limits. Reading about Eurasian jays, wood avens, or red foxes wouldn't have been enough. Seeing them with my own eyes was a completely different experience, one that has

shaped me. We need to see and reflect on our world to better understand it. We should all learn to identify the most common trees, plants, and animals around us just as we learn to read, write, and count. Scientific studies have proven that connecting with nature has positive impacts on our mental health: it can reduce stress, decrease the risk of depression, improve focus, and more.

◇◇◇◇◇

TAKING A CAREFUL, objective look at the wild animals living in a place dedicated to death forced me to re-evaluate the limits of my own world. Like many city-dwellers, I feel an almost instinctive need to be close to nature, and I'm able to satisfy that need every day thanks to the life teeming within Père-Lachaise. I'm far from an expert—I'm still a very amateur birdwatcher, and I sometimes struggle to identify a tree species—but I've learned to give everything the importance it's due, even the invisible or the seemingly insignificant. I've learned that everything has its place. We are all a part of the same world.

One of Père-Lachaise's celebrated residents understood this long before I did. The poet Anna de Noailles authored a body of work that glorifies nature. From Division 28 where she was laid to rest, in a mossy corner of the cemetery thick with undergrowth in certain months, I like to recall the opening lines of her poem "My Offering to Nature." Part meditation and part ode to nature, her words express the vital need that guides us and binds us together.

Sustaining nature from whose bosom all life springs
None have adored you with such passion from their birth
The light of days and all the tenderness of things,
The shining water and the dark and fruitful earth.

I leant against your beauty since my youth began;
Dark forests, mountain pools, the open fertile lands,
These touched my eyes more than the wandering
    looks of man,
I have the odour of the seasons on my hands.[4]

Dying Is Really the Last Thing to Do

I LIKE MORRISON, BUT I prefer Morrissey, the front man of the British rock band The Smiths. The song "Cemetry Gates," off their 1986 album *The Queen Is Dead*, describes a discussion between two friends as they stroll through a graveyard. Morrissey sings:

> So we go inside
> And we gravely read the stones
> All those people, all those lives,
> Where are they now?

I often think of these lyrics as I stroll through my own cemetery. Who were the people whose names are etched into the tombstones? Did they find love? Were they good people? Were they happy? What did they do for a living? Did they have hobbies? Were they able to enjoy their lives? Above all, who remembers them today?

These questions usually go unanswered. Often, just the first and last names appear, along with birth and death dates marking the age at which they died. Widespread religious symbolism makes it possible to intuit their religious beliefs. Likewise, a grave with a square and compass on it suggests the deceased was a Freemason. The shape of the monument itself can provide other clues: broken columns represent a life cut short.

In some cases, an occupation is displayed beneath a name. Failing that, we can look to patterns or decorative symbols, although this is usually reserved for celebrities whose graves double as tribute sites. Alain Bashung's grave features record grooves etched into one corner, and Chopin's is topped with a marble sculpture by Auguste Clésinger depicting Euterpe, Muse of music, holding a lyre. For painters, the palette is often used to symbolize their life's work. Théodore Géricault is represented on his side—the position he painted in after a riding accident left him injured—holding his palette and looking out over bas-reliefs of his most famous work. Great inventors are often laid to rest in tombs that reproduce their inventions: a dynamo generator for Zénobe Gramme and a semaphore telegraph for Claude Chappe. In Division 86, one monument stands out: the mausoleum of animal trainer Jean-Baptiste Pezon is topped by a statue of him riding a lion. Last but not least, the graves of

Père-Lachaise's many military figures frequently feature helmets and weapons.

Occasionally, the circumstances of a death—especially a tragic one—can figure on a tombstone. Flames shoot from the domed memorial of professional balloonist Sophie Blanchard, a nod to the aviation accident that took her life. Similarly, a magnificent statue depicts General Gobert slipping off his horse, mortally wounded, as it rears up into the sky.

◇◇◇◇

WE CAN LOOK to funerary memorabilia either sculpted or engraved on headstones for clues that suggest the place these individuals occupied in society. But even when a monument features an old photo, often a moving one, the deceased's personality—what they loved or hated, what their interests were—remains a mystery.

To find answers, our only hope lies in scouring the epitaphs. These messages, engraved for all eternity, occasionally provide clues as to the character of the deceased they honor. But even then, we must believe them to be sincere. Certain epitaphs, particularly those dating back to the nineteenth century, give us reason to doubt. The fashion of the day was to inflate the virtues of the departed, bestowing them with every quality imaginable: "loving wife," "excellent friend," "pure soul," "faithful spouse," "wonderful sister," "the most righteous of men," "wise woman," "pleasant child," "pious man," "virtuous friend," and the list goes on. An eloquent example of this tradition can still be seen on one grave in Division 57:

To our kind mistress.

The cruel disease that plagued her for so long, that cruel scourge of death, took her from us in an instant. It is painful to see ourselves forever separated from such a kind and respectable boss, she who was always such a good daughter, wife, and mother. Her workers regarded her as a matriarch whose goodness knew no bounds: they bid her a final farewell at the edge of this grave where all life must meet its end. Her memory will remain etched into their hearts for all time.

Farewell, dear mistress. Farewell for all eternity.

Though this period was filled with maudlin epitaphs that exalted the departed, there are, of course, exceptions. The simple yet sublime "Alas!" is still visible on the Loiseau grave just off Chemin de la Citerne. One word says it all. A bit further on, along Avenue de Saint-Morys, one tombstone in Division 50 reads, "Wait a long time for me." Tough love from a widower who was apparently more relieved than heartbroken.

Today, it's no longer in vogue to personalize your grave. Most people recycle standard messages chosen from a catalog and etched into mass-produced headstones so often that they lose their meaning. Here are a few examples of epitaphs you'll find all across France.

Time passes, but memories linger. Who really believes this? As Léo Ferré sang, "With time, everything goes away…"

May your rest be as sweet as your heart was good. Inappropriate when the deceased died of a heart attack. It has a nice ring to it though.

Warbler, if you fly over this grave, sing it your sweetest song. I've never seen so many warbler fans as I have in cemeteries. That said, I like the idea of putting life on a tombstone.

Whatever I do, wherever I go, nothing erases you, I miss you so. Sometimes, lyrics from pop songs do the job. Today, you can find these lines from the hit song "Pas toi" by Jean-Jacques Goldman all over French cemeteries.

Fortunately, personal items left behind on a gravestone can make up for a trite inscription. These include (kitschy) trinkets, plastic hearts, ceramic flowers, pottery, dolls, drawings, poems, and photographs. Occasionally, these keepsakes are scattered over memorial plaques that recall the deceased's hobbies. "Bridge Club misses you," "To André, our beloved boules player," or "Rest in Peace, Your choir friends."

Whenever I walk through Père-Lachaise, I'm always on the lookout for personalized tributes that stand out from the usual platitudes. Though I'm surrounded by funerary heritage treasures, nothing warms my heart like seeing unassuming objects that pack an emotional punch. Like Morrissey, I'm intrigued by all of these lives, and the messages make me feel closer to the people that lie buried beneath my feet. A few simple words can bring tears to my eyes. Some hit harder, especially when the messages are for children. My heart breaks when I see a parent's letter or an older sibling's drawing placed on a headstone.

Certain epitaphs stir compassion, prompt reflection, and inspire reverie. Some will choke you up; others may even make you laugh. The columbarium contains a fairly large number of personalized tributes, as if the lack of a grave inspires families to distinguish their loved one's niche from the others. This is one of the reasons I enjoy walking through the building's cold dark halls. In the course of my wanderings, I always hope to come across another unconventional inscription to add to my list. For example, one niche located in the lower basement reads: "Dying is really the last thing to do." On an exterior niche that doesn't identify the deceased, the inscription reads only: "No means no." Hard to be any vaguer! But my favorite niche is still that of accordionist Jo Privat, whose epitaph features a dark cremation joke: "Here lies one tough cookie."

◇◇◇◇

NOT TO BE OUTDONE, the outdoor plots contain other gems, such as "To my late husband and his beloved wife." Those are some interesting family dynamics! A mistake, no doubt.

In Division 11, you'll find one of the most unique and evocative tombstones in Père-Lachaise: a sculpture of Fernand Arbelot lies holding his wife Henrietta's face in his hands. At the foot of the monument, an epitaph suggests

that the couple loved each other dearly: "They marveled at the beautiful journey that took them to the end of life."

On poet Guillaume Apollinaire's menhir-like monument, visitors have to struggle to decipher the words on the heart-shaped calligram: "My heart like an inverted flame."

Oddly enough, sometimes epitaphs will answer each other. In Division 75, the tomb of writer Pierrette Fleutiaux asks, "Are we going to be happy?" A few divisions further on, along the edge of Chemin Camille Jordan, the grave of writer Marcel Moreau bears the inscription, "I'm happy for the first time in my death."

Others don't shy away from humor, which helps to lighten the mood. Not far from the grave of comedian Pierre Desproges, known for his opening line, "I hope you won't regret coming," writer Jean-Louis Fournier had an ironic message engraved onto the tomb of his wife Sylvie: "In the end, we won't regret coming." On another, the deceased's family thought it wise to note that he'd "died in good health." Ultimately, this is everyone's hope: to die a good death. Rémy Henry, a theater producer who is still alive, engraved his epitaph in advance: "Here lies the producer, but the show goes on." One grieving mother chose the epitaph "Zut de flûte!" (roughly, "Darn it!") for the grave of a son who'd died far too young. Poignant and funny, it can be interpreted as a modern version of the aforementioned "Alas!"

Then there are the epitaphs that make you scratch your head. One example that's been haunting me for months features on a recent plaque: "Who made that decision??? At the Tangier casino, October 6, 2017." I'd love to know what that was all about. Georges Courteline's epitaph is just as mysterious: "I was born to stay young, and I was lucky enough to realize it the day I stopped."

Finally, there are the epitaphs whose timeless truths remind us of our mortality. One example is the line from the Book of Ecclesiastes, "Vanity of vanities; all is vanity." Reading this in Père-Lachaise, a temple if there ever was one to postmortem vanity, may be the ultimate irony. Another chilling example can be found in Division 84:

> To those passing
> Like you I passed
> Like me you will pass

Surrounded by all of these graves and their epitaphs, I occasionally suspend my professional regard and turn my attention to existential questions. What about me? What relationship do I have to my own death? I think about it, of course. Not all the time, but probably more than the average person. I caught the funeral bug at a young age, and fate has put me in daily contact with death as an adult. It's impossible to sweep the matter of my own death under the rug, especially since, as part of my job, I'm regularly confronted with the deaths of people in my generation. They are my age and sometimes share my name. I'm not obsessed with my death, but I am aware that my life will come to an end and that it could happen at any moment. I'm not afraid. My only fear is that I won't have lived enough before I die. Being conscious of my mortality is a catalyst; it fuels a zest for life and gives me the energy and strength to move forward, avoid procrastinating, face reality, and steer clear of victim mentality. Thinking about my own death encourages me to make the most out of life while I can.

What would my grave look like, you ask? I think about that, too, but like many people, I have a hard time imagining it. I think I'd like my tomb to be large enough to hold myself, my wife, and our children—if they so choose. It would resemble a little garden with a small shrub in the middle, where robins could come to nest. A bench would give loved ones or passersby a place to sit. On the headstone, beside a witty epitaph, a QR code would link to my Instagram account so that people could continue to "like" me in death. An empty planter at the foot of my grave would collect rainwater to serve as a trough for foxes and a bath for birds.

In short, I would like my grave to be a place full of life.

Glossary of Funerary Symbols

Funerary symbols have no official definition; they may be interpreted differently depending on the circumstance. Still, here are several common interpretations to help demystify the illustrations at the beginning of each chapter, in order of appearance.

ANGEL. Messengers of God, angels are the intermediary between the living and the dead.

OUROBOROS. The circular depiction of a serpent eating its own tail represents eternity.

INCENSE BURNER. Smoke rising to the heavens is symbolic of the souls of the dead.

PINE CONE. A symbol of eternal life, the pine cone represents the immortality of the natural world.

ANCHOR. Pictured with a broken rope, the anchor represents the end of life on Earth.

PELICAN. Often depicted piercing its breast to feed its young from its own blood, the pelican is a symbol of Christ's sacrifice, as well as of parental love.

BROKEN COLUMN. This symbolizes a life cut short too soon and is often found on the graves of those who died young.

SCALES. A symbol of justice, scales are associated with the Last Judgment.

IVY. An evergreen plant, it symbolizes friendship and eternal love.

FLORAL WREATH. The circle it forms has no beginning or end, representing the cycle of life and rebirth.

TEARS. These droplets symbolize grief and mourning.

CLASPED HANDS. The two hands are a symbol of unity; they represent eternal love and a relationship that survives beyond death.

MASKS. The face contorted in tragedy depicted on theater masks is an expression of pain and sorrow.

OWL. Because they can navigate through darkness, owls are associated with wisdom and intelligence.

BAT. Frightening creatures, bats help guide the soul through darkness.

DOVE. A symbol of peace, the dove also represents purity, innocence, and humility.

SCYTHE AND INVERTED TORCH. The scythe, like the one carried by the Grim Reaper, represents a tool to harvest souls and symbolizes death. The inverted torch represents a life extinguished.

BEEHIVE. Bees are associated with labor, and their hive symbolizes hard work.

PALM LEAF. This symbolizes the glory and honor of those who have distinguished themselves in their lifetime.

BUTTERFLY. With its short life span, the butterfly reminds us of the ephemeral and fragile nature of life.

WINGED HOURGLASS. This symbolizes the passage of time, with the wings guiding the soul toward the heavens.

WEEPING WOMAN. Head covered and weeping over the tomb of a loved one, the woman is an image of grief and suffering.

DOG. Man's best friend, the dog symbolizes loyalty.

◇◇◇◇

COUNTLESS OTHER SYMBOLS can be found on grave markers in Père-Lachaise. Amphorae, for example, are small tear-shaped vessels meant to collect the tears of a loved one.

Religious symbols are also depicted (the Ten Commandments, the star of David, an open Bible, a chalice, etc.) or engraved. You might spot the Christogram, a monogram formed from the Greek letters for Jesus Christ—X and P—often shown with the letters alpha (A) and omega (Ω) on either side, symbolizing Christ's eternity.

Finally, a variety of plants (whose symbolism is detailed in the chapter "The Same World") also appear on graves, making Père-Lachaise a veritable stone catalog of the natural world.

Acknowledgments

I WANT TO START by thanking Édouard Boulon-Cluzel: this book wouldn't exist if he hadn't first contacted me to suggest the idea. I'm very grateful for his revisions and advice throughout the writing process. We saw signs and broke out in a few cold sweats, but it's been an exceptional ride from beginning to end.

Thanks to Jean-Baptiste Bourrat of Les Arènes for his editing genius and for believing in this crazy project, when my "portfolio" consisted of a few Instagram posts. Thanks to the team at Les Arènes, for whom, I'm sure, Père-Lachaise holds no more secrets!

Thanks to my wife, Colombe, who encouraged me during the writing process, read my drafts, and made countless improvements. Thank you for supporting me when the challenge of writing this book racked me with stress and doubt.

Thanks to my own circle of loved ones: my children, parents, brother, extended family, in-laws, and friends.

Thanks to my colleagues and friends Jérôme Ecker and Arnaud Schoonheere, who revised my manuscript and offered advice and feedback.

Thanks to my employer, the City of Paris, for giving me the opportunity to become a cemetery curator. A special thanks to all of my superiors since 2006—Catherine Roques, Pascal-Hervé Daniel, Marc Faudot, and Sylvain École—for their trust and support.

Last but not least, I'd like to thank all of the staff members at the City of Paris Division of Cemeteries that I've had the pleasure of working with throughout my career. They do their jobs with such passion and dedication. Working alongside them is a joy that has nurtured this book.

Notes

1 Honoré de Balzac, *Old Goriot*, trans. Marion Ayton Crawford (Penguin, 1919; Internet Archive, 2017), 304, archive.org/details/in.ernet.dli.2015.149493/page/n301/mode/2up.

2 "Le décret loi du 23 prairial an XII," Résonance Funéraire, resonance-funeraire.com/reglementation/4935-le-decret-loi-du-23-prairial-an-xii.

3 "Victor Hugo—Honoré de Balzac," Victor Hugo Central, gavroche.org/vhugo/balzaceulogy.shtml.

4 Anna de Noailles, "L'offrande à la nature," trans. Sebastian Hayes, Poetry in Translation, June 27, 2012, poetryintranslation.wordpress.com/2012/06/27/click-on-the-link-below-to-listen-to-the-poem-loffrande-a-la-nature-by-anna-de-noailles.

Bibliography

Ariès, Philippe. *L'Homme devant la mort*. Paris: Seuil, 1983.

Barozzi, Jacques. *Guide des cimetières parisiens*. Paris: Hervas, 1990.

Bertrand, Régis, and Guénola Groud, eds. *Cimetières et tombeaux: Patrimoine funéraire français*. Paris: Éditions du Patrimoine, 2016.

Beyern, Bertrand. *Mémoires d'entre-tombes*. Paris: Le Cherche midi, 1997.

Caillot, Antoine. *Voyage pittoresque et sentimental au champ de repos sous Montmartre, et à la maison de campagne du Père-Lachaise, à Montlouis*. Paris: Hénée, 1808.

Charlet, Christian. *Le Père-Lachaise: Au coeur du Paris des vivants et des morts*. Paris: Gallimard, 2003.

Dansel, Michel. *Au Père-Lachaise: Son histoire, ses secrets, ses promenades*. Paris: Fayard, 2007.

Dansel, Michel. *Les Lieux de culte au cimetière du Père-Lachaise*. Paris: Guy Trédaniel, 1999.

Duhau, Isabelle, and Guénola Groud, eds. *Cimetières et patrimoine funéraire: Étude, protection, valorization*. Paris: Ministère de la Culture, direction générale des Patrimoines, 2020.

Healey, Catherine, Karen Bowie, and Agnès Bos, eds. *Le Père-Lachaise*. Paris: Action artistique de la Ville de Paris, 1998.

Horvilleur, Delphine. *Vivre avec nos morts*. Paris: Grasset, 2021.

Langlade, Vincent de. *Ésotérisme, médiums, spirites du Père-Lachaise*. Paris: Vermet, 1982.

Le Normand-Romain, Antoinette. *Mémoire de marbre: La sculpture funéraire en France: 1804–1914*. Paris: BHVP, Agence culturelle de Paris, 1995.

Marchant de Beaumont, François-Marie. *Manuel et itinéraire du curieux dans le cimetière du Père la Chaise*. Paris: Emler frères, 1828.

Michaud-Nérard, François. *La Révolution de la mort*. Paris: Vuibert, 2007.

Moiroux, Jules. *Le Cimetière du Père-Lachaise*. Paris, 1909.

Paix, Camille. *Mère Lachaise: 100 portraits pour déterrer le matrimoine funéraire*. Paris: Cambourakis, 2022.

Raimbault, France. *Le Père-Lachaise: Guide du flaneur*. Saint-Cyr-sur-Loire: Alan Sutton, 2006.

Rheims, Nathalie. *Le Père-Lachaise: Jardin des ombres…* Paris: Michel Lafon, 2014.

Richard, J. B. *Le Véritable Conducteur aux cimetières du Père La Chaise, Montmartre, Mont-Parnasse et Vaugirard.* Paris: Terry, 1830.

Roger père et fils. *Le Champ du repos, ou le Cimetière Mont-Louis, dit du Père-Delachaise.* Paris: Hachette, 1816.

Salomon, F.-T. *Le Père-Lachaise: Recueil général alphabétique des concessions perpétuelles établies dans ce lieu.* Paris: Ledoyen, 1855.

Sergent, Eric. *Symboliquement vôtre: Balade funéraire graphique.* Collection Dilaceratio Corporis. Lyon: Fage, 2022.

Websites

APPL (Amis et Passionnés du Père-Lachaise). *Cimetière du Père-Lachaise.* appl-lachaise.net.

Beleyme, Marie. *Père-Lachaise: 1804–1824; Naissance du cimetière moderne.* perelachaisehistoire.fr.

Beyern, Bertrand. *Pas un jour sans une tombe.* bertrandbeyern.fr.

Landru, Philippe. *Cimetières de France et d'ailleurs.* landrucimetieres.fr/spip.

Pénin, Marie-Christine. *Tombes sépultures dans les cimetières et autres lieux des personnalités qui ont fait notre monde.* tombes-sepultures.com.

Born into a family of grave stonemasons, BENOÎT GALLOT has been the curator of Père-Lachaise Cemetery since 2018. His Instagram account, @la_vie_au_cimetiere, has attracted a growing community of followers captivated by his photographs of the animals that have made the Parisian landmark their home. He lives on the grounds of the cemetery with his family.

◇◇◇◇◇

ARIELLE AARONSON is a French-to-English translator of books, films, TV, and more. Her translations have been shortlisted for the 2023 Governor General's Literary Awards and longlisted for the 2021 Canada Reads book of the year. She lives in Montreal, Quebec, with her husband, their three children, and an ever-growing pile of books.